# 797,885 Books
are available to read at

# www.ForgottenBooks.com

Forgotten Books' App
Available for mobile, tablet & eReader

ISBN 978-1-331-01331-0
PIBN 10133520

This book is a reproduction of an important historical work. Forgotten Books uses state-of-the-art technology to digitally reconstruct the work, preserving the original format whilst repairing imperfections present in the aged copy. In rare cases, an imperfection in the original, such as a blemish or missing page, may be replicated in our edition. We do, however, repair the vast majority of imperfections successfully; any imperfections that remain are intentionally left to preserve the state of such historical works.

Forgotten Books is a registered trademark of FB &c Ltd.
Copyright © 2015 FB &c Ltd.
FB &c Ltd, Dalton House, 60 Windsor Avenue, London, SW19 2RR.
Company number 08720141. Registered in England and Wales.

For support please visit www.forgottenbooks.com

# 1 MONTH OF FREE READING

at

www.ForgottenBooks.com

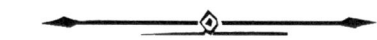

By purchasing this book you are eligible for one month membership to ForgottenBooks.com, giving you unlimited access to our entire collection of over 700,000 titles via our web site and mobile apps.

To claim your free month visit:

www.forgottenbooks.com/free133520

\* Offer is valid for 45 days from date of purchase. Terms and conditions apply.

English
Français
Deutsche
Italiano
Español
Português

# www.forgottenbooks.com

**Mythology** Photography **Fiction** Fishing Christianity **Art** Cooking Essays Buddhism Freemasonry Medicine **Biology** Music **Ancient Egypt** Evolution Carpentry Physics Dance Geology **Mathematics** Fitness Shakespeare **Folklore** Yoga Marketing **Confidence** Immortality Biographies Poetry **Psychology** Witchcraft Electronics Chemistry History **Law** Accounting **Philosophy** Anthropology Alchemy Drama Quantum Mechanics Atheism Sexual Health **Ancient History Entrepreneurship** Languages Sport Paleontology Needlework Islam **Metaphysics** Investment Archaeology Parenting Statistics Criminology **Motivational**

# CHRISTINA FORSYTH OF FINGOLAND

## THE STORY OF THE LONELIEST WOMAN IN AFRICA

BY

### W. P. LIVINGSTONE

AUTHOR OF
"MARY SLESSOR OF CALABAR," "THE NEW OUTLOOK," ETC.

HODDER AND STOUGHTON
LONDON  NEW YORK  TORONTO
MCMXVIII

# INTRODUCTORY NOTE

MRS. FORSYTH, the heroine of the following narrative, lived alone for thirty years in an isolated mission station in Fingoland, South-East Africa, amongst a wild and dissolute tribe of heathens. During that period she never moved outside a radius of twenty miles from her humble mission-house. She seldom saw a white face; she was unknown to the majority of South African missionaries, even to those of the Church with which she was connected; only a few had come across her; fewer still had been at Xolobe. To all who knew of her she was a marvel. The missionary under whom she worked declared that there was not one woman in five hundred who could have lived the life she lived.

Her character was almost as unique as her work. "It is curious," writes another missionary, "that she should have a biography; one can scarcely imagine her reading it. She was simple and unassuming to a degree. Praise was very far from her—she who merited praise more than any of us. We often spoke in admiration of her—but never to her face. In her house, her dress, her speech, her bearing, her surroundings, her whole outlook on life and manner of life, her simplicity and humility and abnegation of self were evident."

Before she retired, at the age of seventy-two, the attention of the writer was drawn to her remarkable career, and he desired to essay some account of it, but waited until she returned to Scotland in the expectation of obtaining abundant material from herself. For the sake of the mission cause she was persuaded to consent to the project, but, when it was undertaken, only grew enthusiastic about her converts, and was smilingly reticent about personal details. What is written, therefore, has been compiled chiefly from an early diary, her reports and letters, and material supplied by friends. Special acknowledgment must be made of the assistance rendered by the Rev. James Auld,

# INTRODUCTORY NOTE vii

M.A., and his sister, Miss E. M. Auld, of Paterson, Kafraria, to whom the book owes much of whatever interest it possesses. When she read the MS., Mrs. Forsyth's only remark was: " There is too much about myself in it."

It is a simple human story. The range of interest and action is a narrow one; no large events or important policies emerge for treatment; the racial, political, and economic problems which bulk so largely in South African affairs find no place in it. But in the whole range of missionary biography one will find few figures who are at once so lovable and so strong, so lonely and yet so happy, so humble and yet so great.

Mrs. Forsyth was very like Miss Slessor, the pioneer missionary of Calabar, in character, faith, humour, patience, and courage, and there are some curious parallelisms in their careers, but the two differed greatly in their methods. Miss Slessor was a worker on a large stage and touched thousands of lives. Eager for territorial expansion she thought in terms of towns and districts. Mrs. Forsyth was an intensive worker, thinking in terms of individuals. To use her own words she was " a watcher for souls." She was as brave and tenacious in seeking to conquer a man or woman as Miss Slessor was to win a tribe.

But it was the same spirit which impelled both, and the service of the one was complementary to that of the other. Hence the record of Mrs. Forsyth's career may complete a picture which Miss Slessor's life began—a picture of how women's faith and love and effort are seeking, along different lines of activity, to redeem and re-create the people of Africa.

# CONTENTS

INTRODUCTORY NOTE . . . . . . v

## PART I

### EARLY LIGHTS AND SHADOWS

I. ARTIST OR MISSIONARY? . . . . 3
II. A LOVE MYSTERY . . . . . . 8
III. FROM FIFE TO SOUTH AFRICA . . . 13
IV. A LAND OF BLOOD AND SUPERSTITION . . 19
V. OVER THE VELD TO PATERSON . . . 30
VI. SCHOOL AND KRAAL . . . . . 35
VII. ON THE EDGE OF REBELLION . . . . 44
VIII. HAIL, RAIN, LIGHTNING . . . . . 48
IX. THE END OF HER ROMANCE . . . . 53

## PART II

### THE HEAT AND BURDEN OF THE DAY

|  |  | PAGE |
|---|---|---|
| I. IN THE DEN OF "WOLVES" | . . . | 59 |
| II. ADVENTURES | . . . . . . | 65 |
| III. THE POWERS OF DARKNESS | . . . . | 71 |
| IV. THE SIEGE OF THE CHIEF | . . . . | 77 |
| V. PERSECUTION | . . . . . . | 81 |
| VI. THE TYRANNY OF TAKI | . . . . | 88 |
| VII. THE WITCH-DOCTOR'S FATE | . . . | 96 |
| VIII. A NINE-DAYS' WONDER | . . . . | 100 |
| IX. THE GREENOCK GIFT | . . . . . | 104 |
| X. OFFICIAL TRIBUTES | . . . . . | 109 |
| XI. AN EXPERIMENT WHICH FAILED | . . . | 114 |
| XII. A FIRE AND A REVIVAL | . . . . | 121 |
| XIII. THE MIRACLE OF TEN YEARS | . . . | 125 |
| XIV. ABDICATION | . . . . . . | 130 |
| XV. THE DOCTOR'S WARNING | . . . . | 134 |
| XVI. VISITORS FROM SCOTLAND | . . . . | 139 |
| XVII. A BIGGER HOUSE OF GOD | . . . . | 144 |
| XVIII. MR. STEWART'S PEN-PICTURE | . . . | 151 |
| XIX. THE NEW UMFUNDISI AND HIS SISTER | . . | 156 |

## CONTENTS

|  |  | PAGE |
|---|---|---|
| XX. Toiling and Rejoicing | . . . . | 161 |
| XXI. Personal Characteristics | . . . . | 169 |
| XXII. A Vision of Souls | . . . . | 177 |

# PART III

## EVENTIDE

|  |  | |
|---|---|---|
| I. Completely shut in | . . . . . | 199 |
| II. Her Independence | . . . . | 204 |
| III. The Shock of the War | . . . . | 209 |
| IV. Sadness of Farewell | . . . . | 214 |
| V. Back to Civilisation | . . . . | 220 |
| VI. Was it worth it? | . . . . | 225 |
| VII. An Estimate from the Field | . . . | 228 |
| VIII. Rest Time | . . . . . . | 232 |
| INDEX | . . . . . . | 235 |

# ILLUSTRATIONS

| | |
|---|---:|
| Mrs. Forsyth . . . . . . | *Frontispiece* |
| Map of South-East Africa . . . . . | xiv |
| | FACING PAGE |
| At the age of twenty-five ⎫<br>A Witch-Doctor . . ⎭ . . . . . | 28 |
| Xolobe . . . . . . . . . | 62 |
| A Group of Fingo Women ⎫<br>A Boys' "Initiation" Dance ⎭ . . . . . | 74 |
| A Typical Fingo . . . . . . . | 102 |
| The Greenock Schoolhouse ⎫<br>Handing over the School ⎭ . . . . . | 131 |
| Married Women outside hut . . . . . | 146 |
| Christian Fingo Girls ⎫<br>A Heathen Family ⎭ . . . . . | 166 |
| 'Smoyana's Bathing Place . . . . . | 206 |

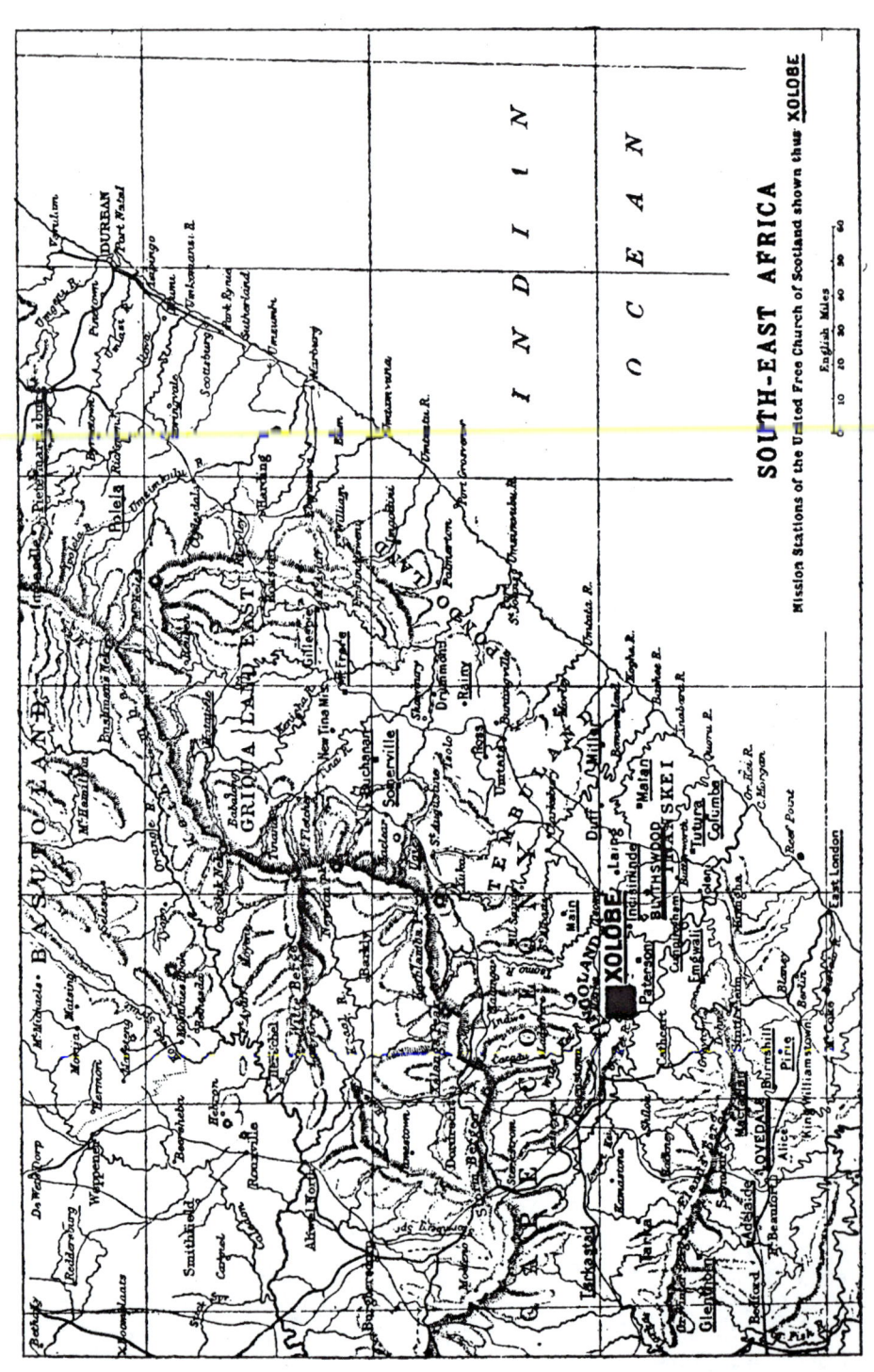

# PART I

# EARLY LIGHTS AND SHADOWS

### Age 1–41

# ARTIST OR MISSIONARY ?

In the early years of last century there lived in Perthshire a prosperous farmer named Moir. He leased two properties—Daldoran and Thornhill—which were well stocked with cattle, and he had a balance of £1000 to his name in the bank. One ill day the laird's factor, a worthless man, who had fallen into difficulties, applied to him for financial help, and he, sympathetic and generous, became his surety to a large amount. As not infrequently happens in cases of the kind, the surety was called upon to make good the responsibility he had undertaken. Ere the claim was satisfied the farmer was swept bare of all his possessions and had not a penny to call his own. The household was broken up, and father and sons went into service.

One of the sons, John, found work in Glasgow. With the same simple trust in human nature as his father he placed all his savings in the care of his master. By and by the latter failed, and John's money was lost. Undaunted, he started again, and after many difficulties and hardships attained success. He was, however, forty-six before he felt justified in marrying. Then came years of sunshine and happiness, with children growing up in the home. There were three girls and a boy, the second of the girls being Christina, who was born on October 23, 1844.

John Moir was a quiet man, of sterling character and deep religious convictions, and his wife was like-minded, and they were loyal to the best traditions of Scottish homes. The children were carefully drilled in the Shorter Catechism, gathering every Sabbath evening round their father and repeating the answers. Often he would tell them that he had learned the Larger Catechism off by heart and rallied them on not being able to do what he had done.

Mrs. Moir died when Christina was ten years of age. The manner of her going was that of one who had lived much in the Unseen. The dividing line had worn very thin. " The room is full of angels," she said, in an awed whisper. She committed the children to the care of Bessie, the eldest, who thenceforward became the mother of the household. Mr. Moir passed away ten years later. He seemed at the last to have a vision of Christ, and his last words were, " Peace. I shall see Him as He is now." The appropriate text of the funeral sermon preached by his minister, the Rev. David Young of Montrose Street (now Woodlands Road) Church, was, " Mark the perfect man, and behold the upright: for the end of that man is peace."

Christina was educated at a private school. She was a girl of original character, taking life seriously, and early began to consider her future. Two careers, widely diverse in character, appealed to her, that of an artist and that of a missionary. She had an eye for pictorial effect, and haunted the city exhibitions. Long afterwards, during the lonely years in Africa, the memory which gave her most pleasure was the enchanting time she spent in those galleries. A cousin who was an etcher encouraged her in her ambition to study art, but her father opposed the idea: in his estimation drawing and painting were not " useful " accomplishments for girls.

The longing to be a missionary was more

deeply implanted in her nature and less objection was taken to the proposal. In her mother, indeed, she found a strong ally who stimulated her interest in the work abroad by every means in her power. The last prayer she taught Christina was, " May the knowledge of the Lord cover the earth as the waters cover the seas."

When she was about fourteen Christina had a definite religious experience which shows how life touches life and creates impulses and movements that influence others in ever-widening circles. A cousin came to visit the family, and one day in conversation she ventured to ask Christina if she had faith in Christ. A simple question, but it startled the girl and made her think. The two friends went to a meeting in Bridgegate Free Church where a workman in his rough clothes told how he had found Christ. " The words that caught me," he said, " were, 'Come unto me, all ye that labour and are heavy-laden, and I will give you rest'." Christina returned home deep in thought and longing to secure the rest and peace which the Divine invitation offered. She knelt in prayer, intimate and intense, and when she rose her life had been surrendered to Christ.

After this she naturally passed into the

service of the Church, becoming a teacher in a mission Sunday School and then in one in connection with Montrose Street congregation. Amongst her colleagues there was a Miss Paterson, who afterwards became the wife of the Rev. John Sclater, the founder of the mission station in South Africa with which Christina became so closely connected. Mrs. Sclater recalls the strong impression which the girl made upon her by her pronounced principles and the character of her prayers at the teachers' meetings. During one of Mr. Sclater's furloughs he gave an address in the church on Kafraria, and so stirred the heart of Christina that she told her elder, Miss Paterson's father, that she was willing to give herself to the work.

## II

## A LOVE MYSTERY

THERE was another experience affecting Christina at this period which had probably the greatest influence in determining her career. The factors that alter the currents of lives are not always visible or known to onlookers; they are sometimes of the most secret character; but it is only in the light of these hidden causes that after-events can be read aright. If the course of true love had run smooth for Miss Moir the African mission-field might have lost one of its noblest workers.

In the church she attended sat a young man, the son of a banker in the city, who was attracted by the fair-haired, winsome girl. The liking was mutual and gradually there grew up between them an affection which ripened into deep and steadfast love. They did not give much expression to their passion; they were both of strong reticent natures; but it flowed pure and sweet and made life for them beautiful and glad. It gave an impetus to the girl's religious impulses and made her a still more earnest and efficient worker.

Time merely accentuated the bond between them. No open declaration was necessary, for the mutual understanding was perfect. The young man went to London to train as a banker and a year or two later he received an appointment in India. He returned to Glasgow to say farewell to his friends. It was not time to enter into a definite engagement, but anxious to keep in touch with the girl he loved he devised a scheme which, he imagined, would fulfil the purpose. He made the three sisters agree to write him regularly and he promised to write each in return. In this way he would be able to correspond with Christina without exciting comment. And so, happy in the dream of youth, he went forth to make his fortune.

The plan was carried out. Christina wrote, and then going quietly about her work, looked and waited for a reply. She waited in vain. Her sisters received letters from India and wrote in return, but none came for her, and she remained outside the friendly correspondence. Her heart grew wistful, then sad, then cold. Gradually all casual references to her dropped out of his communications to the other sisters, and she, on her part, never mentioned his name. It was a mystery. There was clearly a misunderstanding somewhere but she was not conscious of anything blameworthy.

He came home on furlough and they met, but years of silence are not easy to explain or span, and they drifted further apart. She said nothing, showed no sign of distress, and buried her sorrow deeper in her heart.

A poem she wrote at this time gives a clue to her thoughts and fancies. It is like an eyelet in a wall through which we obtain a glimpse into a secluded garden. We see her stricken and disillusioned heart, but we also see her soul rising above mortal pain and struggle and finding peace and rest in the Eternal. We see also the blossoming of those qualities of faith and devotion which sent her at last to Africa in obedience to the " golden law of sacrifice " :—

> Wherefore, O wav'ring soul, this wild unrest,
> This beating at the prison bars of life ?
> It is the Lord of All who dealeth out
> Thy daily lot—how canst thou then repine ?
> Think of the sorrows of the Lord of All,
> His daily dying through His earthly years,

## A LOVE MYSTERY

The agony of dark Gethsemane,
When blood-sweat flow'd, when darkness fill'd His soul,
With none to watch and none to sympathise.
Behold thy Saviour drink the bitter cup
Unmurmuring—" 'Twas not My will, but Thine."

Think, think of this, my soul, and how canst thou
Say aught ? Think of false Judas ; remember too
The soldiers, with the lanterns and the staves ;
The Spotless Lamb led silent forth to slaughter ;
The malice and the fiendish craft of men
And devils all array'd in blackest hate ;
The garments parted, and the kingly robe,
The reedy sceptre, and the crown of thorns
Piercing His flesh ; anew the blood flows forth.
And all that pain and shame were borne for thee.
And now they blindfold, mock, and buffet Him ;
Then force the weary, fainting Son of Man
The heavy cross to bear, along the way
Of grief to Calvary, where He, uplifted, dies
With basest ones on either side. My soul,
Behold the Man ! my soul, behold thy God !
This death brings life to thee. And now
Combined is all the force of Hell. The sun
In horror seeks to hide his face, and noon
Doth wear the sombre hues of darksome night.
Christ in deep anguish cries : " My God, My God,
Why dost Thou Me forsake ! " 'Mid pangs of death
Resigns His soul into His Father's hand,
And then 'tis o'er. Triumphantly the cry
Utter'd on earth is by angelic hosts
With gladness caught and echoes through all space
As they do bear the Lamb of God again
To Paradise, with ransom'd new-born soul,
Pledge of His pow'r to save to th' uttermost,

Baffling the very might of Satan,
As He arose, the first-fruits from the dead.
My soul! thou canst not fathom love like this.
It has a height, a depth, a length, a breadth
Thou canst in life but know in part; but joy
Awaiteth thee. Look up, rejoice, He lives,
A glorious Saviour! Constantly He pleads
For thee within the veil, with God, thy God.
Thy times are in His hand, He orders all—
Joy in the thought that thou canst suffer loss
Or cross for Him. He led the way, He bids
Thee follow on, and with thy life it ends.
If it is dark, how bright the light of heav'n,
Pure, dazzling, unimagined and unknown
To mortal earth. Here night shuts out the day,
" Earth's fairest flow'rs bloom but to fade and die,"
And fondest friends forsake. He felt this too.
Cling close to Him; He will not leave in life
Nor yet at death forsake. Him glorify;
Let every wish, and word, and work be for Him,
And for those who love His name; and those
Who are without bring in that they too may
Receive His saving grace. The golden law
Of God is sacrifice. The fields are white
To harvest, but the labourers are few—
Lord of the harvest, thrust Thy lab'rers forth.

. . . . . .

Fear not; the cloudy pillar leads by day,
The fire by night; beneath the brooding cloud
The manna falls, and He is " God with us."

. . . . .

Yea, as the boundless ocean covers all
The deep, so shall the knowledge of Thy name
O'erspread the earth.

# III

## FROM FIFE TO SOUTH AFRICA

ALL thought of the mission-field was meanwhile banished by the call of a service lying more closely to her hand. John Moir was, in accordance with his mother's wish, studying for the ministry, and one of the sisters was needed to keep house for him. Christina saw that this was the path of duty for her and cheerfully subordinated her own ambition to his interests. John passed through the High School, University, and Divinity Hall, graduating M.A. and B.D., and was called to Cairneyhill, in the west neuk of Fife, whence his sister naturally accompanied him. She was now a capable young woman of twenty-eight, in every way fitted to discharge the duties of the lady of the manse.

Cairneyhill is situated in the historic district where the Relief Church was cradled, and borders the high road from Dunfermline. The manse and church stand side by side, two plain grey buildings, with a garden and a neighbouring " green " still known as the tent-green, because the preaching tent was pitched there at the sacrament season.

The manse of Cairneyhill was well known throughout the United Presbyterian Church, for in it had been carried on, during the ministry of the Rev. John More, a " seminary for young ladies," which drew pupils from all parts of Scotland. Its founder and principal was the minister's wife, who, for forty years, both taught and mothered the girls with equal efficiency. The hospitality of the manse was proverbial, and there was seldom a week-end when some distinguished preacher or group of college students did not pay it a visit. Mr. More was a man much beloved by his people, and when Mr. Moir settled amongst them he found his memory still cherished. His own modest and gentle ways reminded them so much of their old pastor that they slipped into the habit of calling him " Mr. More," and " Mr. More " he continued to be to the end.

Nothing seemed more circumscribed and permanent than the life Miss Moir lived in this quiet country manse, yet the lines of coincidence were stretching out from the ends of the earth to change its even tenour.

# FROM FIFE TO SOUTH AFRICA 15

One day there appeared a young mining-engineer named Allan Forsyth, the eldest son of the editor of the *Inverness Advertiser*, who had just returned from Australia and was paying a visit to his aunt in the village. He was attracted by the pleasant thoughtful woman flitting in and out of the homes of the people and he wooed her diligently. She regarded him with favour. That old romance of hers had still tremendous power over her inmost feelings, but it was foolish to cherish the thought of it and make it spoil her future, and so she resolutely put it away and turned to the practical possibilities of life. Before long the friendship culminated in an engagement, but as Mr. Forsyth was called away to some work in South America, the wedding was deferred.

In due time John Moir married and his sister felt free to realise her old longing. She had always been attracted by the character of the work in South Africa, where both the Free Church and the United Presbyterian Churches carried on missions amongst the Kafirs, and in 1878 she offered herself to the Mission Board of the United Presbyterian Church as an unpaid worker for that field, for a period of three years. In view of her attainments she was accepted as a teacher for the girls' school at Emgwali, the mission station rendered famous by its association with the first ordained native minister, the Rev. Tiyo Soga. Started in a thatched cottage in 1861 by the Ladies' Kafrarian Society, an auxiliary Church agency which has, during its long career, rendered splendid service in the cause of education in Kafirland, the school developed into a well-equipped and efficient institution, and became noted as a centre radiating Christian and civilising influences amongst the natives of the country.

Thirty-four years of age, Miss Moir was older than the women missionaries who are now taken on the staff, but she never saw cause to think that she began too late. It might be very well for younger girls to undertake ordinary station work, but she believed that in the case of the difficult conditions and problems associated with raw heathenism, age and experience count more than freshness and enthusiasm.

She left Southampton in the s.s. *Nubian* in January 1879, the month when the Zulu War opened so disastrously. The first part of the voyage was very stormy, and there was a great deal of sickness amongst the passengers, but calm came in time. The company on board was a varied one, and there was much to interest and amuse the untravelled but observant and shrewd Scottish passenger who kept so quiet and tranquil amidst the petty distractions of the journey.

In her diary are brief characterisations of various persons: the Bishop who was kept busy all day escorting the numerous seasick ladies of his party on deck, and who preached to a pale and listless few from the text, " Man goeth forth to his work and to his labour till the evening"; the Curate who threw off his sanctimoniousness when he threw off his surplice; the German who was so desperate to learn English that he waylaid ladies for lessons; the bejewelled diamond-digger and gambler who said there was no proof that the Bible was true, and who, on being told to think half an hour daily, declared that if he were to think he would go mad; the children to whom she found gingerbread cake an excellent means of introduction; the lady who told her, a little spitefully, that she had seen more degraded people in Edinburgh and Glasgow than in the whole of Natal.

After a passage of twenty-four days Cape Town was reached. It was bathed in the light of sunset, and Miss Moir thought she had never seen a lovelier sight. Here she made her first acquaintance with the dark-skinned natives, and set herself, as she said, to "get used to them." At Port Elizabeth she visited the places of interest, but everything suggested "a thirsty land wherein is no water." The steamer arrived at East London, the port of entry for the vast territory of Kafraria, late on a Saturday evening, but a storm kept the passengers on board until the following afternoon, when she was swung over the side in a basket, and landed and faced alone the strange conditions of a new country.

## IV

## A LAND OF BLOOD AND SUPERSTITION

ON the way out she had been studying books relating to South Africa—Theal's chiefly—and taking notes, endeavouring to form some conception of the country to which she was proceeding, the people who occupied it, and the conditions of life amongst them; and gradually she built up a picture in her mind which had greater elements of interest than she had imagined. She knew that the sub-continent of Africa was classic mission ground, but she began to realise that the whole story of its human occupation was extraordinarily fascinating and thrilling, an epic of movement over vast regions in which entire races strove for mastery and survival, a record of struggle, adventure, and peril, and that the district in which she was being located was the scene of some of the most dramatic episodes in the development of events.

\* \* \* \* \*

As she read, a vision of the country came before her, and especially Kafirland itself, rich in physical beauty and economic possibilities. It lies in the eastern corner of South Africa, where the coast curves round from the Cape and is washed by the warm waters of the Indian Ocean. From the sea the land rises in a series of terraces until it culminates in the lofty range of the Drakensberg.

Into this strip of territory is crowded a wonderful throng of valley, wood, plateau, veld, and peak, threaded by streams and rivers, now low and quiescent or altogether dry, now pouring down in sudden flood. A pastoral and agricultural country, the chief productions are sheep and cattle, maize, oats, wheat and barley, and potatoes, beans, and other food plants. Only small patches of the soil, however, are cultivated by the natives.

The seasons are the reverse of those in Britain, summer extending from October to March, winter from April to September. In the district of Fingoland the summer is uniformly hot, often with a shade temperature of 100 to 104 degrees, and there are frequent thunderstorms and hailstorms, but the mornings and evenings are cool and exhilarating. In winter there is a dry sunshiny cold, the temperature often falling below 45 degrees, and the higher hills are white with snow.

\*     \*     \*     \*     \*

Then her thoughts dwelt on the history of the land. South Africa was originally occupied by the Bushmen, a pigmy people on the lowest level of existence, but with some idea of art, as drawings of animals on the walls of their cave dwellings testify. They were succeeded by the Hottentots, who, though wild and savage, were superior to them both in physical and mental qualities. Their language had peculiar suction " clicks " made by the tongue against the teeth or palate and used for the sound of certain letters.

Both Bushmen and Hottentots dwindled almost to the point of extinction before the advent of a stronger race, composed of many groups calling themselves the Bantus, who swept in great waves down from the unknown north. The vanguard of the advancing horde moved along the south-eastern seaboard, and overran the whole of the fair country as far south as the Great Fish River, where it came up against the frontiers of the white men. To the members of this, the Xosa group, was applied the name of Kafir—an Arab word meaning "unbeliever"—and the region became known as Kafraria.

The Bantus were a nation of warriors who acted on the principle that might was right; they entertained nothing but contempt for tribes who were weak and loved peace, and crushed them without pity; and those whom they enslaved they exploited without mercy. From the Hottentots they adopted the "clicks" which form so curious an element in their speech to-day.

Whilst Cape Colony was being settled and developed—with an occasional clash on the barderland between the forces of civilisation and borbarism,—events were taking place in the interior of the continent of the most appalling character. In one of the more powerful Zulu groups a lad named Chaka grew up, active, daring, and ambitious. Step by step he rose to command the army, and eventually became ruler of the tribe. He was in his rude way a military genius, he devised the short assegai, trained and disciplined his warriors into perfect efficiency, and organised schemes of colossal conquest.

When all was ready he began a course of systematic subjugation, rapine, and slaughter. He ravaged the continent from east to west, laying waste populous regions and exterminating entire tribes, including vast numbers of women and children. Historians estimate that from first to last nearly two million lives were butchered or starved to death through the agencies he set in motion.

Many tribes fled before the approach of the destroyer, and in their turn plundered and murdered as they marched. One of these was the wild Angoni, who finally settled on the high lands of Nyasaland, now a mission-field of the United Free Church. Another group, consisting of broken remnants of several tribes who concealed themselves in the forests and subsisted by cannibalism, at last crossed the Tugela River, and made their way down through Kafirland, where in 1824 they were attacked and defeated by the Xosa. *Amamfengu* they were called—" vagrants, wanderers"—a word which Europeans soon twisted into Fingo. They were so cowed by their experiences that they had no spirit to resist the harsh and humiliating serfdom which was imposed upon them. Events proved, however, that in submitting to the yoke they were unconsciously stooping to conquer.

There was no cessation of the frontier troubles with the Kafirs, who periodically raided the Colony and left a trail of fire and blood behind. The missions of the Free Church and United Presbyterian Church of Scotland and other bodies stood as outposts in a sort of no-man's-land and were subject to perpetual alarms and often destroyed. Punitive expeditions were undertaken, but the Imperial Government were reluctant to add to their responsibilities by acquiring more territory.

During one of these campaigns the Fingoes begged to be taken under British protection, and about 17,000 were located south of the Fish River in order that they might form a buffer region between the two races. As with the negroes in Jamaica and the Southern States of America, the bitter experiences of slavery had destroyed many of their tribal customs and taught them habits of regular industry, and when they regained their independence they developed rapidly in character and material prosperity. This was specially the case when they came under the influence of the missionaries. In subsequent wars they proved their loyalty and fought well for the Government. British officers referred to them as holding prayer-meetings in camp and as being an example to the white soldiery.

The event which more than any other brought the long struggle for supremacy to an end was one of the most extraordinary in the history of Africa. It was a case of national suicide. A seer, prophesying through the medium of his niece, announced that orders had been received from the spirit-world that the Kafir people were to kill their cattle and destroy their maize and corn. As soon as this was done vast herds would emerge from the ground, the country would smile again with grain, and there would be luxuries, clothes, and guns for every one. The warriors of the past would reappear, and in a final conflict, the whites and the Fingoes would be scattered like autumn leaves and swept into the sea. All who believed this, and acted in the faith of it, would enjoy perpetual youth.

It was a glittering prospect—but the cost! The Kafir loves his cattle and it tears his heart to part with them. There was, however, no escape. The paramount chief, Kreli, ordered every man to obey, and the work of destruction was carried through to completion. Over two hundred thousand head of cattle were killed and the entire corn supply was scattered to the winds.

When the time for the fulfilment of the prophecy passed and the days wore on, the Xosa passed through agonies of anxiety, fear, disappointment, and despair. They were in a land without food. Impelled at last by hunger and misery they began to crawl into Cape Colony, a nation of skeletons, multitudes falling dead by the way. Fully 30,000 men, women, and children perished. In a short time the country beyond the Kei River—the Trans-kei—was depopulated and deserted, and nothing but empty kraals and heaps of snow-white bones were left to tell the tale of a people's magnificent faith and incredible folly.

The policy of the Imperial Government was still against the extension of colonial territory, and the desolated upper part of the Transkei was, therefore, offered to the Fingoes. They flocked over in their thousands. Many Christians were amongst them, but also some of the worst characters that heathenism develops. These naturally kept together and settled in out-of-the-way districts.

It was thus that Fingoland came into

## A LAND OF BLOOD 27

existence. Missionaries of the Free Church and the United Presbyterian Church at once followed up the migrants, and divided the region into two zones of influence. The Rev. Tiyo Soga, then missionary at Emgwali, chose a site in the United Presbyterian sphere for a station among the Christians who had settled at Mbulu, and the work of organising and establishing a mission was entrusted to the Rev. John Sclater, who came from Scotland for the purpose. This station soon became well known throughout the Church at home. To Mr. Sclater succeeded first Major Malan, a Christian soldier, and then the Rev. James Davidson, who went through the last Kafir war in 1877, when four United Presbyterian stations were plundered and destroyed. Though Mbulu was only a few hours' march from the scene of hostilities, Mr. Davidson stuck fearlessly to his post, as also did his Free Church neighbour at Cunningham.[1]

\* \* \* \* \*

Of the people in their present condition she knew only what was told discreetly in the books. There was much to their credit.

---

[1] In this story the term Mbulu is applied to the district, and the station is given its recent name of Paterson after Mrs. Sclater's uncle, the Rev. Dr. Paterson of Kirkwall.

A brave, robust race, proud and independent, and possessing abundant intellectual ability, they appealed to her own strong nature. Though they had lost their tribal government and many of their habits had been modified in contact with civilisation, they had changed little in essential character and the great bulk were still heathen.

They lived, she learnt, in kraals or villages of beehive-shaped huts constructed of wattle-and-daub or sods, with only one low opening, which served as door, no chimney, and little or no furniture. Formerly they clothed themselves with the skins of animals, now they wore blankets which they folded gracefully over their bodies, and they adorned themselves with necklets and armlets of beads, and copper and iron rings. As a protection from the sun and insects they rubbed their skin and blankets with red clay mixed with fat, hence the name "red" Kafir; when they became Christians the clay and the blanket were renounced in favour of civilised dress. Polygamy prevailed. Women occupied an inferior position, being bought in marriage for a dowry of stock, and a man calculated his wealth by the number of wives and cattle he owned.

Her chief interest was in their religious

AT THE AGE OF 25.

A WITCH-DOCTOR

## A LAND OF BLOOD 29

position, and she gathered that though their folk-lore showed considerable powers of imagination they had never reached forward to any true spiritual conceptions. What might be called their religion was a hazy mixture of magic and mystery. The Unseen to them was peopled by malignant spirits, and their lives were haunted by superstitious fears which were played upon, for his own profit, by the witch-doctor or priest.

Some of their tribal rites were repulsive in the extreme, and virtue under the conditions imposed by custom was impossible. But such a general statement conveyed nothing to her. What it really meant she was to learn, to her horror, in the days to come.

# V

## OVER THE VELD TO PATERSON

Knowing no one in East London Miss Moir made her way to the nearest hotel. Next day she went down to the Custom House to secure her luggage. As she stood in the crowd she heard some one say, " I've been looking a' day for a Miss Moa-r, and I'm blowed if I can fin-nd her."

She turned and saw a young man. " I'm Miss Moir," she said, smiling.

Instantly his manner changed; he became extremely polite, and stated that he had been sent by Mr. Coutts, the agent of the steamship line, to find her. Mr. Coutts, a Scot, was known as the " guardian angel of the missionaries " on account of the kindly interest he took in their welfare. He looked after the affairs of new arrivals, arranged their journey into the interior, and saw them off by train. To his care Miss Moir gratefully committed herself.

# OVER THE VELD TO PATERSON

Early in the morning, without breakfast, she boarded a train for Peelton, thirty-eight miles up country. At the first stoppage she felt the need of food and asked the guard how long the train waited. "Oh," he said, "just till you're ready," and she had therefore time for her cup of tea. With her usual helpfulness she carried another cup to her sole fellow-passenger, a decent country woman with a babe in her arms, and was presented in turn with a rosy-cheeked apple which, somehow, brought up a memory of Scotland.

From Peelton she proceeded over the veld by bullock wagon to Emgwali, a garden on the rolling expanse of bare country, and was received by the Principal, then Miss Ogilvie, who was called by her Kafir girls "the mother of the sorrowful." The new teacher was warmly welcomed by the native women—amongst whom were two widows of Sandilli, the famous chief of the Gaika tribe, who had taken part in the last rebellion. "Sometimes," they said, "we feel inclined to doubt the goodness of God, but we thank Him for sending another teacher. We did not know we had so many kind friends over the sea."

She continued the task of acquiring the language with the quiet resolution habitual to her. Kafir is not easy; it is more difficult than the Efik spoken in Calabar though not more difficult than Chinese or the tongues of India. It was odd to hear it spoken and sung in all its native vigour by the people; owing to the " clicks " in many of the words it seemed as if she were listening to a collection of clocks ticking or a body of carters starting their horses.

She found that her name was a stumbling-block. There is no sound of " r " in Kafir—the word Kafir itself is foreign to them—and they could not pronounce " Miss Moir " but they soon turned it into "Miss Moyana " or " 'Smoyana " by which she was ever afterwards known. As Moyana means " a breath " (in a spiritual sense) or " a little breeze," it was not an inappropriate designation for one who was destined to come into their lives so often like a breath of pure air from the fields of God.

She had not long, however, to sit and hear the strange " *ba, be, bo,*" of the children at their lessons. Word came from Paterson that Mrs. Davidson, the wife of the missionary, was seriously ill, and that a helper was urgently required. Miss Moir was chosen to go.

Travelling all day through a rain-washed

land bright with geraniums and aloes she camped after sunset, gipsy fashion, and next morning crossed the Kei River in a wagon drawn by fourteen oxen and arrived the same evening at Paterson.

The beauty of its situation appealed to her. The station stood on a slight eminence at the head of the Mbulu Valley and commanded a far-stretching view down towards the Tsomo River and away to the mountains about the Kei. High hills, that suggested to her the slopes of Arran, enclosed it, with richly wooded glens softening their lower outlines. Here and there, in open spaces, or half-hidden by vegetation, the round huts of the natives clung to the ground like limpets to the rocks on the shore. From the heights immediately above a magnificent prospect was obtained as far north as the Stormberg Range. The manse, a little below the church, was a goodly building with a garden stocked with orange and other fruit trees and flanked by singing streams.

So, in the ordering of her life she came to the district where her work in the future was to lie. But there were years of training and hard experiences to be undergone before she finally settled in the niche that was waiting for her.

Those who remember her at this time state that she was very cheerful and happy. She evinced a high conception of duty and had evidently surrendered herself completely to the service she had chosen. Strongly built, slow and deliberate in speech and manner, she impressed them as one who would persevere steadfastly in whatever task she undertook and would never deviate from it because conditions did not square with preconceived notions. How true the estimate was her subsequent career will show.

# VI

## SCHOOL AND KRAAL

HER advent at Paterson synchronised with an event which she always remembered with pleasure. She had not been more than a day or two in the manse when the Rev. Dr. Laws, then engaged in founding the Livingstonia mission in Nyasaland, paid the Davidsons a visit. The famous missionary gave an address to the Christian and heathen population in which he told them a little of his life-story, described the work of exploration and settlement in which he was engaged, and asked for men to assist. Two natives offered themselves as evangelists.

Perhaps what struck her most at first was the extraordinary amount of work devolving upon the missionary. He had a population of from nine to ten thousand under his care: there were many outstations, one thirty miles away, one twenty-five miles, another twenty miles, a fourth eleven, a fifth ten and so on; the day schools numbered nine with 550 scholars, the Sunday schools ten with forty-nine teachers and 452 scholars. The mountainous nature of the country added greatly to the difficulty of travelling and the fatigue incurred in supervising his vast "parish," and it was always a wonder to her how he compassed all he had to do. Yet his was not an uncommon case. in the South African mission-field.

She soon learned, also, to realise how potent a force the missionary's wife was in a South African mission-station, and to have compassion on her. The missionary had his varied travelling and intercourse with teachers, agents, and visitors to keep his spirit fresh, but upon the wife lay the monotonous burden of domestic management, and the handling of a thousand and one irritating details. Often there were hardships of no ordinary kind to be endured, involving risk to strength and health, but the difficulties and trials were faced and overcome with uncommon courage and cheerfulness.

The advent of a white teacher, trustworthy and efficient, brought great relief to Mr. and Mrs. Davidson. She was entrusted with a large part of the day school work in

## SCHOOL AND KRAAL

conjunction with the native teacher. There was an average of sixty scholars but the numbers soon doubled. They were the children of Christian and heathen parents and attended in all sorts of attire. Most of the boys wore long shirts; some had jackets but no trousers. One was arrayed in a soldier's old coat, and all displayed brass rings. The girls came in prints and shawls and without shoes or hats. The latter were taught sewing and knitting in addition to the ordinary subjects.

The school was not without children of an older growth. One six-foot lad strove hard to keep dux of his class. Another "boy" twenty-four years old, and married, came thirty miles to attend the white teacher's reading lessons. Such ambition did not seem unnatural to Miss Moir after she had talked with a man who offered her £5 if she would teach his child to be a good arithmetician.

"I will do it without a premium," she said. "But why are you so anxious about it?"

"I went," he replied, "to the white man's shop to buy a blanket, and was made to pay 16s. for it. Afterwards I found a ticket on it which I was told was marked 10s. I want my boy to read so that he may not be cheated when he grows up."

" Very well," she agreed; " but he shall be taught something for the life to come as well as for this one."

Coming out of the " red " huts, the children were often in an unfit state for school and a dozen at a time would be sent down to the river to be cleansed. Their quaint ways were a perpetual source of interest and amusement. A little household girl, when her turn came to repeat a verse from the Bible, thought a moment and said, " God loves me; me loves God." " Where is that found ? " she was asked. " Oh," she replied, " me make it up; me in a hurry; not time to learn."

Even at so long-established a station as Paterson the desire to take advantage of the school was by no means general. Many heathen parents placed it under a rigid boycott and threatened to beat their children if they ventured near.

There was one girl with a gentle voice and kind disposition who attracted the teacher's attention by her eagerness to learn. She was the daughter of a heathen and had, when an infant, been thrown out to die by her grandmother because she seemed too

## SCHOOL AND KRAAL

sickly to live. Her cries caused her mother to crawl out and bring her in, and she was nursed into strength, and was now a fine healthy girl of thirteen. Her father proposed to remove her from school, and in dread of the blow she one day shyly asked her teacher to visit him. His hut was on a plateau at the end of the valley with a magnificent view. She found him to be a tall muscular man, clad in a blanket, seared and worldly, and afraid lest Bekiwe would not wish to be sold for cattle when she came of age.

Miss Moir thanked him for allowing the child to attend school.

"I didn't send her," he said roughly, "she went herself," adding significantly, "when these clothes are done where is she to get new ones?"

"If Bekiwe trusts in God He will provide for her."

Some time afterwards Bekiwe received a shawl from a Sunday School in Scotland, and she said to Miss Moir, "'Smoyana, you said if I trusted in God He would provide, and He has sent this."

In a letter of thanks to the children of the Sunday School she said: "My parents are heathen, I am a believer, but they are not like me, believing. The place I live at is the place where the heathen sit. I am the only person who dresses."

"What made you think of going to school?" her teacher once asked her.

"When I looked at my father's pass," was her reply, alluding to the written permission to travel obtained by natives from the magistrate, "I thought I would like to read it and so decided to come to school for a year. God came into my heart and then I had no wish to leave."

Of Bekiwe we shall hear again.

Another important work Miss Moir undertook was to visit the kraals on Sunday mornings accompanied by a bodyguard of the Christian children who formed a kind of choir. In this way she came close to heathen life in its stark squalor and degradation, and to the heathen mind, so curiously simple and yet so bafflingly complex.

Not always was she welcome. Some men, when they saw her coming, would slink away up the mountain — "to look after their sheep," they said. One exclaimed in disgust, "You are always speaking about your gods. I am sick of it." Another muttered, "God will be with us whether we love sin or not." After she had spoken on the resurrection,

## SCHOOL AND KRAAL

one protested indignantly, "*I* will not rise from the dead." The only comment of a young man on an address she gave on prayer was, " Can I get what I want from God ? "—then, in an undertone, " I would like a jacket."

This materialistic attitude of mind sometimes had startling manifestations. One day she was sitting in a kraal in the midst of a group of half-naked men and women decked with ornaments of beads and coins. They were cooking, eating, or lounging, while lean dogs roamed around. She began to tell them the story of the Crucifixion. As she spoke the women fastened their eyes upon her, their hearts touched by the pathos of the great world-tragedy. When she finished they expressed their horror at the cruelty of the men who had put so gentle a Saviour to death. Then one young man, covered with beads, rose, and with dramatic posturings showed how He had hung on the Cross and suffered and died.

She never lost patience with them. Quietly, doggedly, unceasingly, she taught them the love of God and the principles of the redemptive gospel. When she asked one man what he would do with his child if the latter would not come to him or obey him, he said: " I would speak pleasantly to it and induce it to come." "That is what I mean to do to you until I bring you to the Great Father," was her reply.

" Never mind the people not treating you kindly, 'Smoyana," remarked another man. " They are ignorant and foolish, and know nothing; go on and teach them."

From time to time a wave of spiritual conviction and surrender moved the district and swept considerable numbers into the membership of the Church. These occasions often followed prayer-meetings which were held by the people themselves and were carried on throughout the night.

One evening the women of the Church met for prayer in a Fingo hut. Mr. Davidson and his daughter and Miss Moir went over and entered, and sat with the natives on the floor. The place was dimly lighted by a candle and a lamp, and in the rows of dark, intent faces they saw many of the school children. Some of the women were in tears; one grew so excited that she overturned the lamp. When the missionaries left at ten o'clock the meeting was in full progress.

In the early hours of the morning Miss Moir was awakened by the sound of weeping, and discovered that it came from the people,

# SCHOOL AND KRAAL

who were marching in the darkness from the hut to the Church. Many were in deep distress and crying out to God. At half-past four Mr. Davidson and Miss Moir went up with candles, and the missionary held a short service and then advised all to go home. They left, but gathered again in the hut, and continued until morning in prayer. Some hours later, when Miss Moir was in school, which was held in the Church, the women who had been at the meeting entered the building. School was dismissed, the bell was rung, and another prayer-service was held. Mr. Davidson asked all who wished to give themselves to Christ to stand up, and forty did so.

On another occasion the church bell was heard ringing at one o'clock in the morning. Mrs. Davidson and Miss Moir rose and went to the church, and found a company labouring under great excitement. Men were on their knees praying fervently. One was huddled at the door weeping. A woman in heathen dress with a baby on her back cried aloud, " Lamb of God, take away my sins ! " Mrs. Davidson addressed and quieted them, and they gradually dispersed.

# VII

## ON THE EDGE OF REBELLION

The country had never quite settled down to conditions of peace, and there were occasions when the outlook caused anxiety. One night when Mr. Davidson was at an outstation, and Mrs. Davidson and Miss Moir were alone in the manse, a wild cat endeavoured to gain entrance into the fowlhouse. At midnight Mrs. Davidson arose and opened her window and shouted in the endeavour to frighten the animal away. Then fearing that Miss Moir would be alarmed she went to her room and explained.

"Oh," was the calm reply, "I thought the rebels had come and were murdering you, and I was just waiting my turn!"

After the Zulu uprising the Cape Government thought it wise in the interests of peace, to disarm all natives throughout the country. The Basuto tribe refused to comply with the requirement and hostilities ensued.

## ON THE EDGE OF REBELLION 45

The disaffection extended to the territory adjoining Fingoland, occupied by the Tembu and Pondomisi clans, the boundary of which was only three hours' ride from Paterson.

Towards the close of 1880 rumours of rebellion began to reach the manse. The Fingoes grew alarmed, for in such racial conflicts they were always classed with the Europeans. " What can we do ? " asked a woman. " We have been disarmed. The minister will need to pray hard for us."

Then news came of a magistrate having been treacherously slain, of white traders and Fingoes being murdered, of shops being plundered and wrecked, and of refugees escaping over the border. All available forces were mobilised, and mounted police patrolled the district. As an attack was expected, the party at the manse were ordered to be ready for instant flight. They buried their valuables in the garden, made up a change of clothes, and placed their coats and ulsters where they could be swiftly picked up.

Mr. Davidson, however, was unwilling to leave unless he were driven out by force. He had been through one war already, and was not afraid. He held communion and took as his text, " Should such a man as I flee ? " " I prefer," he said, " to die at my post of duty." When the levies departed for the front the women of the district went up to a mountain overlooking the rendezvous to watch and pray.

From the out-station of Lutuli, within an hour's ride of the enemy, came a request that Communion might also be dispensed there before the men left for Tembuland. Mr. and Mrs. Davidson at once responded to the appeal, and Miss Moir accompanied them. They found a large company gathered, including many heathen, with badges on, ready for action.

As the service proceeded, a little girl, the daughter of the chief, tiptoed into the church, and approaching her father who was officiating as an elder, whispered something in his ear. He rose and went up to Mr. Davidson.

" Make haste," he said, " a mounted messenger has brought word that fighting has begun and we must go."

The heathen men left the building, and saddled the horses while Communion was dispensed, the chief performing his duties as calmly as on an ordinary occasion.

Then the women gathered round their husbands and sons and bade them " Goodbye." There was no sighing or sobbing.

## ON THE EDGE OF REBELLION 47

then, but when the company had passed out of sight they came together to weep and pray.

On the way back to Paterson the missionaries saw huts burning on both sides of the border, and encountered many fighting men hurrying to the scene as well as Fingoes fleeing from the enemy country.

Some hours later the women of both stations met, and ascending a high hill remained there in intercession from sunrise to sunset.

The missionaries were perpetually on the alert, but the news that was brought of the progress of the operations became less alarming. Shortly after the paramount chief of the Tembus had set fire to a mission-station he was killed, and the conflict slackened. Then other chiefs surrendered, and the war was over. The Mbulu contingent returned without loss.

# VIII

## HAIL, RAIN, LIGHTNING

The work of the station resumed its normal course, the only disturbing events being the occurrence of droughts, floods, and storms. Hailstones on one occasion broke most of the windows in the mission-house. The dry spells were particularly trying; so high did the temperature sometimes rise that even the natives were injuriously affected. Prayer-meetings for rain were usually held at such periods, and Miss Moir's testimony as to their effect is remarkable. Once, for instance, a drought was being experienced, suffering was imminent, and a day of humiliation and prayer was appointed by the chief magistrate of Fingoland. The morning was sultry and intensely hot, the wind blowing as from a furnace. At a kraal near the station Miss Moir held a service, and told the people of the efficacy of genuine intercession. An evangelist began fervently to

## HAIL, RAIN, LIGHTNING          49

pray that the drought would break. As he went on, a peal of thunder was heard, rain began to fall, and Miss Moir was drenched before she reached the manse.

After a period of scorching heat a thunderstorm broke over Mbulu. The lightning played vividly about the station, and the thunder crashed and rolled with long reverberations down the valley. After one terrific peal came the cry, " The church is on fire ! " There was a rush to the building, but the natives were afraid to venture near. When rain began to pour down an attempt was made to save some of the furnishings ; one man seized the clock, another the Bible and copy-books, others the seats and door ; but all else was consumed.

It was a disaster, but not irremediable. The people at once resolved to proceed with the erection of a new and better building. With the self-denial which has always been characteristic of the Christian members of the tribe, they gave freely of their time, labour, and money. They quarried the stones and provided oxen to convey these to the site. They offered gifts large and small. The children brought every penny they saved. Two boys of ten who went a long day's journey with a message received

E

a shilling for their trouble. Tired and hungry, they appeared at the mission-house and asked for two sixpences in exchange. Next morning at school they tendered a sixpence each " to build the church." Bekiwe received 1s. 6d. to provide herself with a new jacket. Before going to buy it, she also handed in a sixpence.

When the foundation-stone was laid, a horse, sheep, and other live-stock were cheerfully given. The spirit of the people was amusingly shown by a competition which took place between a native teacher and his mother-in-law. She put down a penny. He laid down a threepenny piece. She capped it with another penny. He placed a threepenny piece on that. And so the friendly contest went on until her tenth and last penny was gone; but not to be outdone, she went and brought half a dozen eggs and set them down.

Contributions in kind were often given to the mission. A woman once appeared with a pot and bundle on her back. She laid down the pot, lifted the lid, and let out four chickens. Then, opening the bundle, she released the mother-hen, saying: " Take them; it is my offering to the Lord." When the church at the out-station of Incisininde

## HAIL, RAIN, LIGHTNING 51

was opened, one teacher gave £1 for himself and a sheep for his boy; another, a clock; a third, window-blinds; a fourth, pennies equal to the number of his scholars—120. A heathen chief in Highland cloak and earrings said: "I give a sheep for my first wife, a sheep for my second wife, a sheep for my third wife, a sheep for my fourth wife, and a sheep for myself." Many gave again and again. The total amount received on that occasion was £120.

\* \* \* \* \*

The three years for which Miss Moir had engaged herself were at an end. According to Mr. Davidson she had done splendid work, and he was sorry to lose her. So were the people. They came to bid her farewell, giving her " tickies "—threepenny-pieces—to keep them in remembrance. One of these was also sent to their old missionary, Mr. Sclater, with a message: "*Abahlolokazi baka Esigubudweni ba - bulisa Umfundisi Slatelli pesheza kolwandle, kakulu* "—" The widow women of Esigubudweni greet Rev. Mr. Sclater over the sea very much." Two little boys in shirts shyly presented her with a shilling, " to buy food for the way."

She received two quaint addresses, one from the scholars, 115 in number, and one from the teacher. The latter, referring to her " humble heart," said " Miss Moir was so kind that I had almost forgotten she was a white person. She didn't show any difference in colour for the whole of the three years she was here." He praised her for being so good a mother to the " little dirty Fingo children," and then he drew a picture of how " their little eyes " would be gazing away in the direction of Kei looking for the return of " their good kind Miss Moir—in vain."

# IX

## THE END OF HER ROMANCE

SHE reached Scotland to find her old romance risen, like a ghost from the past, to mock her with the thought of what might have been. The mystery of the broken relationship had been solved. The explanation was simple and no blame attached to the lovers. It had been a case of jealousy and intercepted correspondence.

The banker learnt the reason when it was too late. To his dismay he found that she was engaged to Mr. Forsyth, who now came from South America to claim his bride. The tragedy of unfulfilled dreams was hastening to its close.

After spending a time at Cairneyhill Miss Moir was married to Mr. Forsyth in Glasgow, and the couple went to reside in London. But the lure of the gold-fields continued to draw the mining prospector. At this period the Transvaal was coming into notice as a gold-producing area. The first really successful field in South Africa was that near Lydenburg—rich alluvial ground from which nuggets many pounds in weight were being unearthed. Mr. Forsyth made up his mind to try his fortune there, and a few months later the couple were settled at the picturesque mining town among the mountains.

Their married life was brief. Little more than a year afterwards Mr. Forsyth was fording the Komati River on horseback when his saddle shifted in mid-stream, and he was swept away by the flood-waters and drowned. The news was broken to Mrs. Forsyth by two members of the Dutch Reformed Presbyterian Church, the elder of whom slipped into her hand a paper on which was written, " Thy Maker is thy Husband."

Her life again seemed to lie in ruins about her, but there was one bright gleam in the darkness. She received a letter from her former lover offering her a home with his two sisters. Though deeply touched by his thoughtfulness and devotion, she felt she could not accept his bounty, and he acquiesced. A few hasty lines which he sent her reveal his poignant sorrow and resignation:

> We may not meet to tell the tale
> Of all our griefs and fears,

# THE END OF HER ROMANCE

> To mark the ravage time has wrought
> Within three dreary years.
> We may not meet in this cold world
> But we shall meet above,
> And for the pains we've suffered here
> We'll reap abundant love.
> We may not meet to tell the tale
> Of those we trusted long ago,
> Who stood by us in times of peace
> But left us in our woe.

It may be added that some years later, having retired in ill-health, he died in Edinburgh. Thus ended our heroine's one real romance, though its memory, at once bitter and sweet, had always power to move her strong, reserved nature to its depths.

\* \* \* \* \*

She faced the future with a brave heart. Her income would only be £40 per annum, and it was not possible to do much on that. She could, of course, return to Scotland and spend the remainder of her days in some narrow and obscure position; but her nature craved a less conventional outlet, and her thoughts turned longingly again to the mission-field. She would never be able to emulate the missionaries, with their extensive spheres and great range of service, but she felt in all humility that she might be able to fill a niche somewhere—perhaps undertake the kind of work a Biblewoman did at home. She was willing to go forth, not knowing or caring whither, and make her home alone in the desert with only the heathen around her.

A letter was soon on its way to the Mission Board of the United Presbyterian Church in Scotland offering her services as a voluntary worker for Kafraria. She made it quite clear that she would ask nothing from the resources of the Church.

"I should not like to displace any worker now engaged," she wrote; "I only wish to help the cause of God with my time, influence, and means. I will go where there is the greatest need, where a missionary is away on furlough, where there is a missionary family in sickness or trouble, or where there is an out-station with native chief without a missionary. If the Board will point out the place where my time will be most usefully employed, I am ready at once to go and begin."

So fine and disinterested an offer was accepted with gratitude, and she was asked to go, in the first place, to Paterson. Selling her house, she returned by the new route through Portuguese East Africa to Delagoa Bay, and thence to East London and Paterson, which she reached early in the year 1886.

# PART II

# THE HEAT AND BURDEN OF THE DAY

### Age 41–67

# IN THE DEN OF " WOLVES "

MR. AND MRS. DAVIDSON were glad to see their old assistant once more. Her face was shadowed by the suffering of her experiences, but her smile was as calm and sweet as ever. They hoped she would settle down into her former work, and were disappointed to hear that she had determined on a new line of service. She wished, she said, to be placed alone in some out-district in connection with the mission—preferably the most backward region—where she could have a definite bit of work to do and be responsible for it.

There was no need to discuss where that was. The thoughts of the missionary at once travelled to it—Xolobe[1] about ten miles away to the north-west, an isolated " pocket " of heathenism between the Xolobe and the Kei Rivers. He recalled the route to it—the long stretch through a rocky cañon,

[1] The " X " in Xolobe is pronounced with a click.

the steep climb up the mountain-side covered with scrub, the rough ride through open country, the descent by sheep- and cattle-track into another valley, and then the little knob of ground with the dark circular huts of the natives mottling the landscape round.

Half-jestingly he said, "Well, there is Xolobe."

"Send me there," she replied.

He looked astonished.

"But," he remonstrated, "you know what it is—a wild region of unbroken heathenism. The people are the off-scourings of the emigrant Fingoes whom degradation and badness have kept together. 'Wolves,' one of my elders calls them. For years I have wrought there with some of my best agents but have made no headway amongst the rude and barbarous population. They are lazy, liars, and notorious thieves. Again and again I have tried, and again and again, on account of the opposition, I have had to close the school and leave the place to itself. It would never do for you to go there alone."

"I will go at once," she said. It was exactly the kind of service which appealed to her faith and courage.

He regarded her thoughtfully. She was

strong and capable, a woman of experience—she was now forty-one years of age—and knew her own power and capacity for holding out. It was possible that she would succeed where others had failed.

He made one more objection.

"It would be a poor sort of life for you; it would be very lonely; it would be giving up too much."

But she only smiled as knowing better, for she thought of some lines by Dr. Walter C. Smith which she had learnt by heart and were a kind of motto guiding all her actions:

> All through life I see a Cross
> Where sons of God yield up their breath;
> There is no gain except by loss,
> There is no life except by death.
> There is no vision but by faith;
> No glory but by bearing shame,
> No justice but by taking blame:
> And that Eternal Passion saith,
> "Be emptied of glory and right and name."

Her confidence impressed and fortified him. The longer he thought of the idea the more it appealed to him, and at last he decided to let her go.

When the project became known to the scattered European residents strong disapproval was expressed. They thought she should not be permitted to take the risk of living alone in such an isolated and wild locality among a degraded class of natives addicted to the worst practices of heathenism.

Mr. Newton O. Thompson, the magistrate of the Tsomo district, was much concerned on her behalf, and wondered whether it would be wise to allow her to carry out her wish. "The majority of natives," he writes, "belonged to the class known as 'reds.' To make matters worse many of these people had no desire to be interfered with, and consequently regarded the coming of a lady-missionary into the location with suspicion. Some were much addicted to beer-drinking, and on such occasions were anything but pleasant neighbours."

Mr. Davidson, however, said that his own doubts had vanished and he thought there need be no anxiety as to her safety, and this settled the matter.

Packing her baggage into a wagon and taking one of the Paterson elders with her she set off, and, after a toilsome journey, arrived at Xolobe. Surveying the conditions of the district, she saw that all Christian work and influence had gone to pieces, and standing in the midst of the moral desolation her heart sank within her. She wondered . . .

XOLOBE.
From a water-colour sketch by Miss Auld.

## IN THE DEN OF "WOLVES"

" How many Christians are there ? " she asked the elder.

" One," he replied.

Taking her Bible, she turned over its pages thoughtfully and read in Ezekiel :

"*The heathen that are left round about you shall know that I the Lord build the ruined places, and plant that that was desolate : I the Lord have spoken it, and I will do it.*"

And then there came into her mind a vision of Xolobe won for Christ, and from that moment she never faltered.

A lover of nature, she was helped by the beauty of her environment. The mission reserve was situated on a lip of land surrounded by majestic precipices and steep hill-sides covered here and there with patches of woodland or bush, and was almost completely isolated by a couple of streams which, after a series of minor falls, met and flowed on to join the Great Kei River. Down the valley her eye rested upon high hills faced with rugged rock, clustering kraals, fertile fields, and herds of cattle and flocks of sheep and goats tended by native boys. The scarlet aloe relieved the sombre greens by its splashes of brilliant colour. As the fleeting changes of light and shadow settled into the soft tones of evening the fierce and naked fronts of the heights were lit up with glory, orange and rose and purple, and then all suddenly faded into the darkness and stillness of the night with wreaths of white mist trailing mysteriously in the dimness and lights glimmering here and there through the open doorway of huts.

She lay down that night in a Kafir hut on the tops of the boxes she had brought with her, and covered herself with a shawl. But she could not sleep, and was early up and about in the morning. Xolobe in the soft clear light looked to her "a gem of beauty," and with a more buoyant spirit she began that patient service which was to last, without pause or respite, for thirty years.

# ADVENTURES

Her first task was to become acquainted with the people and get into touch with the children, and so introduce an atmosphere of confidence that would prepare the way for settled work in school and church. Remembering Tiyo Soga's words that as a race the Kafirs prefer to be drawn, not driven, she made no stir, used no pressure, but moved about quietly, with soft speech and observant eyes, talking with this one and that one, and silently laying her plans. She had the patient, persistent, imperturbable manner characteristic of the true African pioneer, that unresting, unhastening movement which we find best exhibited in the " forward tread " of Dr. Livingstone.

Her method was to visit the huts, carrying some simple medicines with her as a sure means of winning an entrance. She would appear suddenly in some kraal where the men were sitting, wrapped in their terra-cotta blankets, smoking and gossiping, give them a pleasant word, and enter the nearest hut, stooping through the low doorway from which the smoke was issuing. A wife, red handkerchief on head, would be attending to the evening meal. The fire occupied the centre, and upon it would be set a pot containing Kafir corn, while a boy or girl, clothed only in a necklace of beads, would perhaps be roasting mealies from the cob. She would find out the circumstances of the family, talk sympathetically about them, and then read and pray.

The faith of the sick in her powers was pathetic. One old blind man besought her to lay her hands upon his eyes and restore his sight. "That power," she said to him, "belongs to God alone: but I can show you how you can get the eyes of your soul opened."

Sometimes she would address the groups in the open, but the painted men looked upon her only as a diverting curiosity. Some were polite and interested, some scowled, others were indifferent. When she read the Bible, told them about Christ, and prayed, they laughed. To them her religion

# ADVENTURES 67

was absurdly childish, and they treated it with amused scorn.

Far and wide she went. No journey was too long or toilsome if sick folk called for her services. She was asked to go to a spot which a native evangelist had told her was inaccessible. "There are no roads to it," he assured her. She quietly gathered what was necessary and set out. On the way she passed a hut where the children ran terror-stricken from the sight of a white face.

Some of the places were twenty miles away, too remote to be visited in one day, and she had often to spend nights in the kraals. A message from a big man called Gaka took her to his home on the flat of a mountain top. A steep path bordered by wild geraniums, zinnias, and gladioli led to it. In a hut Gaka's mother was lying sick of a fever amongst dirt and squalor. 'Smoyana chased out the noisy children, did what she could for the comfort of the sufferer, and read and prayed. Then she gathered the boys and girls about her and taught them. A man came in and was interested in her talk; he had never heard of God and did not know who He was.

At sunset the women returned from their "gardens," or fields, where they had been at work since daybreak, and set about making the evening meal—Kafir corn, pounded and boiled, served with amasi or sour milk. This was the hour of gossip, and the man who did not know God kept the company shaking with laughter by retailing the scandal of the day. 'Smoyana, however, created her opportunity, and spoke to them of deeper things. After prayer she was glad to retire to a hut where the women, the children, and a couple of kids were her companions. She slept on a mat with her clothes on. At dawn she left for another long journey to attend some sick children.

In these early days her position was not free from peril. One Sunday afternoon she was at a distance from Xolobe when a thunderstorm threatened and she turned her steps homewards.

In a lonely hollow amongst the hills two strange men appeared from amongst the scrub and began to follow her. She felt instinctively that they meant mischief and, turning, she eyed the one who was nearest, a tall powerful fellow whose blanket was slung over his shoulder and who carried a huge club. His face was that of a fiend; she thought she had never seen so repulsive a creature.

" You seem to be in a hurry," she said.

" What have you got there ? " he demanded.

" Bibles."

Remembering that she had been told not to allow a native to walk behind her if she feared violence, she commanded him to go on before. He did so but kept near.

Looking behind, she observed that the other man had come up noiselessly and was at her back. She felt a thrill of alarm and looked round for a way of escape. At that moment a local native suddenly appeared out of a path above them driving cattle. Her expression of relief made the men turn, and seeing the herdsman they scowled and after a moment's hesitation made off as quickly as they had come.

When Mrs. Davidson was told of the incident she remarked, " They meant to murder and rob you, of course," a surmise which was subsequently confirmed.

One Sunday she had been attending the Communion at Paterson and had been detained, and it was five o'clock in the afternoon ere she left to trudge the ten miles back. Darkness fell but she kept on. At last she lost the roughly-defined track and went wandering amongst the rocks and scrub. It was impossible to tell where she was, and she abandoned the attempt to proceed and took shelter for the night behind a boulder. The hours passed slowly; she wearied for the dawn. With the light she discovered that she had been resting on the edge of a precipice. One step more and she would have been killed.

She tramped to Xolobe and took up her duties as if nothing had happened.

# III

## THE POWERS OF DARKNESS

In her going in and out amongst the people she came more closely into contact with the conditions of primitive native life than she had hitherto done. Outwardly she found them picturesque enough.

The majority of the Fingoes were not black but dark brown in skin, and their bodies, shining under the fat and red ochre or clay rubbed upon it, looked like polished bronze. The blanket was the sole article of clothing of the men, and even this was often thrown aside in warm weather. It was greased and coloured in the same way as their skin and embroidered with blue and white beads. The dress of the women was a skirt fastened round the waist, with sometimes a shawl wound over the upper part of the body and a coloured handkerchief or fillet round the head. Both men and women decorated themselves with necklets and armlets of beads, shells, copper, ivory and wild beasts' teeth, and the men usually carried a knobkerry or stick.

The women drew out her sympathies in a special degree. There was much simple dignity about them. As she met them with their babies tucked into a fold of their blankets on their back, or carrying head loads of wood or green maize and other produce, she admired their symmetry and grace. But they were practically little better than chattels, being acquired in marriage by the highest bidder of stock. This is a custom which, on account of some advantages it possesses in existing circumstances, is not altogether condemned, but is bound to disappear under the continued impact of Christian ideals. The wives were the real workers in the native hive, being not only domestic drudges but all-day toilers in the fields, while their husbands only performed some perfunctory tasks and lounged and smoked. Often cheerful enough, their faces had that look which one usually sees in non-Christian lands—the patient but lustreless expression as of an unawakened soul, which contrasts so notably with the bright and intelligent aspect of Christian womanhood.

## THE POWERS OF DARKNESS 73

Involuntarily, however, she penetrated deeper beneath the surface of native life, and saw heathenism in all its naked effrontery, and then she began more fully to realise the tremendous difficulty of the task she had undertaken. It was the rites and practices of centuries she was challenging.

The system of religion she did not fear; it was merely a superstitious belief in goblins, demons, and ancestral spirits, which, potent enough in its practical effect on their lives, would gradually disappear before the light of the truth.

Nor did she dread the witch-doctors, men often of great cunning and ability, always a powerful influence for evil, who played on the weakness and follies of native nature, and terrorised young and old.

What she did fear was the terrible hold which the tribal customs had over their bodies and souls.

There was, first of all, polygamy, regarded partly as a tribal duty in former days to maintain the fighting strength of the armies, but an arrangement appealing to the self-indulgent sense of a barbarous people. It created a formidable obstacle to Christian discipleship, for, when a man wished to join the Church it meant that he must separate himself from all his wives save one, and there were obvious hardships involved in such a proceeding. Many would have gladly accepted the gospel from the first if they had been allowed to retain their wives, but the law of the Church was inexorable and though they might be hearers they could not be admitted to membership.

But polygamy was as nothing to the hideous initiation ceremonies through which every boy and girl had to pass into the stage of manhood and womanhood. In the case of the lads there was the rite of circumcision, which, in itself, was not by some very seriously objected to, but it was associated with practices of the most immoral character. During the process of initiation these novitiates were covered with white clay and dressed in grass skirts and masks. In the case of girls *intonjane* ceremonies marked the corresponding period of isolation.

No description of the rites is possible; it is sufficient to say that when the young people emerged from their course of " training " and license they had lost for ever that innocence and purity which are the beauty and the crown of life.

Another curse was beer-drinking. No doubt it was the only method by which the

A GROUP OF FINGO WOMEN

A BOYS' "INITIATION" DANCE

natives could give expression to their social instincts, but it led to every kind of viciousness and immorality. Much of the time of the women was taken up with preparing the drink—in beating and grinding the corn, and making, boiling, and straining the stuff. In her visits to the kraals Mrs. Forsyth came across many a carousal. The people were gathered together in huts, which were crowded to suffocation, each man and woman taking long draughts of the liquor amidst a babel of confused talk and laughter. This would go on for days and nights, whilst the children went neglected or unprovided with food.

Such were the peculiar evils which our heroine found entrenched in the district she had come to evangelise. When everyone, young and old, was steeped in sensualism, what hope was there that she, one lone woman, could work a saving change? How could she stem the raging current of uncleanness flowing as fiercely and irresistibly as a river in flood?

She shivered as she thought of it all and of her own helplessness, but she took refuge in the assurance that with God everything is possible, and relying on His guidance and help she braced herself for the struggle.

She passionately desired to succeed. " I ask Xolobe for Christ," was a pathetic sentence in one of her reports.

Her greatest weapon was prayer. She was not content with petitions in general terms, but made definite intercession for particular persons, and she begged her correspondents to follow the same plan. " I ask for prayer for so and so," was the burden of her letters. In a poem which appeared in the juvenile magazine of the Church she voiced the cry of the children of Xolobe to the children of Scotland :

> *We* lie outside the Shepherd's fold—
> The night is drear and dark and cold,
> While *you* are safe and warm within,
> Guarded and fenced and hedged from sin,
>   *Oh pray for us !*

" Oh pray for us," was her cry to the end.

## IV

## THE SIEGE OF THE CHIEF

HER most stubborn fight was with Mnyila, the chief of Xolobe, a typical " red," conforming to all the customs of his tribe with the fanaticism of a zealot. He set a bad example to his people who were frequently embroiled in tribal fights. On one occasion the affray was so serious that the authorities arrested and imprisoned his followers in a body, and fined them to the extent of £100. This sum was promptly paid, but the punishment did not stop the vendetta. A kraal near the mission-house was surrounded by a wild body of men, who attempted to stab the police sergeant despatched to arrest them. Afraid for Mrs. Forsyth's safety, an old heathen came and said to her :

" Ma, these bad people of yours like to fight ; you must rise up and go away from them."

" But," she said, " if they are bad they

need me to stay and help to make them better."

From the first Mnyila avoided her, would not go near her meetings, and forbade his people to go. His principal wife Nomonti was of the same mind. It was one of her huts which 'Smoyana was occupying, and she used often to come in and talk to her about the strange manners and customs of the white people across the sea. A very clever and intelligent woman, she parried all the missionary's frontal attacks and would have nothing to do with her religion.

But it was the chief himself to whom 'Smoyana laid siege with the deliberation and determination of a general assailing a fortress. She paid him surprise visits, and when she caught him talked to him with uncompromising directness, denouncing his sins, and at the same time persuasively presenting the better way. He listened with genial equanimity, and when she left turned with added zest to his revelries.

Once she found the kraal folk engaged in indecent dancing. The chief kept out of her way; the others turned a deaf ear to her reproofs. She approached the head wife:

"Why are you doing these dreadful things on God's Sabbath day?" she asked.

## THE SIEGE OF THE CHIEF 79

" Ma," was the reply, " you do not understand; if we do not observe our customs sickness will come upon us."

'Smoyana opened her Bible. " This is God's book," she said, " and He says this " : —fearlessly quoting accusing passages and throwing them at her like bombshells.

The chief's eldest son was often present when 'Smoyana attacked him ; he had some conception of the truth, and once he was so overcome by the visitor's solemn admonitions that he burst into tears and left the hut. 'Smoyana had hopes of him, but he, too, shrank from the surrender of his heathen practices ; the sacrifice was too great.

She was well aware how difficult it was for these men to change their manner of life ; it involved their whole social status and future. A native lost his position in his tribe when he abandoned the customs of his fathers ; there was a heavy pecuniary sacrifice in the abandonment of polygamy. Those who renounced the initiation ceremony were considered apostates to tribal tradition and virtue, and treated with contempt and derided as " boys."

But she realised that a beginning must be made, and that every convert rendered it easier for others to take the step, until the time came when a Christian community could be formed and Christian ideals dominate the land. To win a chief would be a great victory, and the influence of such an event would spread far and wide. She never, therefore, grew tired of trying to save Mnyila, though he continued to make determined attacks with the object of suppressing her work. Once, too cowardly to come himself, he sent his brother with the plain intimation that he would be glad to see her leave the district. She ignored the request, and merely redoubled her efforts to storm his pagan heart. No case was hopeless in her eyes. And she had her reward. He became less hostile, and at last sent her a message :

"Speak much to my people, 'Smoyana, and teach men about God, because we are all wrong."

Imprisoned for theft, he was deposed. Afterwards he became very ill, and, much softened, he humbly accepted Christ and died converted. Matole reigned in his stead, a heathen, but more favourable to the mission work.

# V

## PERSECUTION

It was in a small wattle-and-daub building which had been erected in the time of Mr. Sclater that Mrs. Forsyth gathered the few who were weary of their old ways and brave enough to seek after better. Though uphill and often disheartening work, her courage and lovingkindness never failed, and one after another of the people dropped in and became interested and friendly. One heathen actually presented her with a threepenny-bit to help the cause. She sent it to Scotland with the remark: " Perhaps this red man's offering may make some of the people at home who give pence and halfpence to the collection try to give a little more."

But when she ventured to open a day-school in the same building the opposition broke out afresh, and she encountered endless difficulties and disappointments. The local witch-doctor was her most powerful enemy, and incited the whole district against her.

"Heathenism is rampant," she wrote to her friends at home. "Darkness covers the earth and gross darkness the people. Imagine seventeen children in one family whose father hinders them from attending school, but is ready to allow them any sinful indulgence. When I expostulate with them they say: 'We do not know it is sin; our parents teach us these things.'"

But again her quiet persistence wore down all hostility; in twos and threes the children began to attend, and soon she had seventeen girls and fifteen boys, whom she taught writing, arithmetic, geography, and grammar, imparting also to the girls some knowledge of sewing and general housework. They came in red clay attire, a *bayi* or cotton sheet which the boys wrapped round their bodies, and the girls tied at the waist with a straw cord, fixing it below with buckles into a kind of petticoat.

They were wonderfully eager to learn, and many walked long distances and arrived footsore and weary. Perhaps it was the singing that attracted them, for all Kafirs, young and old, are passionately fond of music, and they enjoyed nothing so much as

## PERSECUTION

the learning of the Kafir hymns 'Smoyana taught them—those simple melodies which appeal to Christian children all over the world.

But the teaching had its effect. When visiting a heathen kraal she asked if a little boy who came to the school ever spoke about anything he learnt there. " Yes,": replied his mother, " he takes his elder brother aside at nights and says, ' Let us pray.' "

Perhaps, also, it was the singing as much as a feeling of curiosity, which drew the parents from their work in the fields to watch the strange proceedings in the little mud schoolroom. Some of these thought that whatever the motive of the white woman was, the effect on the children appeared to be good, and they good-naturedly allowed them to go; but the majority, jealous for the maintenance of their old ways, continued tacitly to oppose the new development. Periods of persecution recurred, during which the school had to be closed. Attendances often mysteriously dwindled, puzzling the teacher until she noticed that the falling away always happened after some boy or girl had expressed a desire to be a Christian. The first lad converted was handed over to the tender mercies of the witch-doctor and forced to renounce his faith. When four scholars made an open confession that they had accepted Christ, every "red" child was taken away on some pretext or other.

"It is a bitter trial," she said, "but we cannot lower our standard. We never conceal our intention, which is, to win Xolobe for Christ."

Then the imposition of a school tax by the Government annoyed the people and revived the antagonism, and the most promising pupils were withdrawn. Other interruptions occurred. An outbreak of fever stopped the work for months, many of the natives and their children fleeing from the district in terror of the epidemic. "Still," she wrote, "we have reason to thank God and take courage. Amidst all our weariness and shortcomings we know and feel that He is with us."

"She is working away," wrote Mr. Davidson at this time, "in a spirit of indomitable courage and perseverance. I found her as hearty as ever in a school full of children. A child has been the means of converting the mother, and I baptized them both. It is one of the darkest parts of the land where I could make no headway till she took it in hand."

## PERSECUTION

In 1889 she added the fiftieth name to the roll. " I trace all this," she said, " as an answer to prayer."

One day when she had been fighting difficulties a passing stranger looked in. " Do you remember me ? " he asked smilingly. " I am one of your old scholars at Paterson." He was now the second teacher in the largest school in Fingoland. She had a long talk with him, found that he had been loyal to his training, and always sought to lead the children in his care to Christ. His visit was like a gleam of sunshine in a grey day, and she returned encouraged and invigorated to her task.

Along with the day school she started a Sunday School, but this, on account of the early morning hour at which she held it not suiting Kafir domestic arrangements, was not at first so successful. Finding that many girls remained about the station in the interval between the Church services, she formed a midday Bible Class for them, which came to fulfil very much the same purpose, and was one of the most important features of the work. None gave her such pleasure and satisfaction as this class of raw girlhood, over none did she brood with more loving and wistful concern. How she toiled to bring the young lives into the safe keeping of her Lord! How she brought her simple and absolute belief in the efficacy of prayer to bear on each doubtful or anxious case!

In these early days there were three members in particular whom she desired to convert—Jane, Bertha, and Daisy, all about the same age. They were regular in attendance and learnt their lessons well, but they would not make the change over to a Christian life. 'Smoyana employed every means in her power to bring them to a decision but in vain, and, completely baffled, she was almost in despair when she remembered the answer given to her by a lady speaker at home whom she had asked to reveal the secret of her power. The reply was, "This kind goeth not forth but by prayer and fasting." She chided herself for not realising this sooner, and at once put the principle into practice. She fasted a whole day and continued in prayer on behalf of the three girls. In the following week Jane, the most obstinate of the trio, came alone to the candidates' class and signified her desire to accept Christ. Then when the class met the other two followed her example.

Such incidents, added to conversions amongst women and boys, alarmed the

## PERSECUTION

heathen community, and a common effort was soon on foot to stop the secessions from tribal use and wont. Women were beaten by their husbands again and again because they would not renounce the profession of Christ which they had made. Two sisters had their clothes taken away to prevent them attending the meetings, but they appeared in scanty undress. When they returned to their homes their indignant mother cried, " Go away; we don't want *qobokas* (Christians) to live with us." Another girl was scourged by her uncle and thrown out of the hut. Mrs. Forsyth took her in and tended her with a mother's care. Boys also had their clothes and wages seized when they showed themselves attracted by the new way of life.

Our heroine had a fierce hatred of injustice, and the courage of her convictions, and she welcomed and protected every runaway who fled to her. The station was at this time a sanctuary for the outcast and oppressed.

# VI

## THE TYRANNY OF TAKI

THE story of one typical family may be given to illustrate the extraordinary ferment going on in the district, and the trials which the converts, like the early Christians, had to suffer at the hands of the persecutors.

Taki was a caretaker in a store which was mysteriously robbed during his master's absence. The thieves were never discovered. Taki, however, lost his post and looked unhappy as if he had something on his mind. 'Smoyana made a point of visiting him frequently but he resented her solicitude.

" Speak to others," he said gruffly, " but do not speak to me."

" *Whosoever shall not receive you nor hear you, when ye depart, shake off the dust under your feet for a testimony against them,*" she quoted, and rose and left.

She had not gone far before she heard the

## THE TYRANNY OF TAKI

daughter running after her calling her back. " He bids you return," she cried.

When she reached the hut she received a grudging apology.

The daughter, Nomnyaka, a good-looking girl of marriageable age, was eager to know more of the truth but was afraid of her father. One day she bought some cotton sheeting and began making clothing. Her father came in, gave her a look, and seized a sjambok. She fled out of the hut, down to the mission-house, he pursuing her with the whip. Mrs. Forsyth was out, but the housegirls let her in. The father stopped at the entrance. When Mrs. Forsyth arrived she found the girl trembling and in violent fear. She kept her at the station, provided her with clothes, and gave her work to do in the garden and house, and she joined the girls at school, attended the meetings, took part in family worship, and was perfectly happy.

By and by a brother-in-law, a witch-doctor, took up her case, invited her to go to his house, and promised to allow her to wear clothes, and freedom to worship God and attend school. When the father heard of this he promptly came and made the same proposal; naturally he did not want to lose the *lobola* or dowry he would receive when she married, which often amounts to ten head of cattle. His offer she accepted, and returned home, and later was baptized and took the name of Kate.

A Christian widower from another outstation then took a fancy to her and they were married in Xolobe Church. She made a good and industrious wife and a capable mother.

At the marriage a girl in red clay stood outside, curious to see the ceremony, but refusing to go in. She watched the proceedings through the open window. It was a half-sister of Kate called Raqula, the daughter of Taki's second wife. Mrs. Forsyth knew her as one who had never been permitted to come to school, and was never seen playing about like other children. When at her hut one day she asked her, " Wouldn't you like a doll to play with ? " " No," was the child's reply, " I like to make the house nice for mother," and went on with her task of pounding and beating the clay floor to make it smooth and clean.

After the marriage of Kate further disturbances occurred in the family. Raqula's mother was converted, and through her influence her step-mother and sister were

## THE TYRANNY OF TAKI 91

also brought in. Her punishment was severe. She was driven ruthlessly away, all her fowls and belongings were sold, and a new wife was installed in her place. Raqula was glad to leave the home and live with a heathen man some distance away.

One Sunday morning a young woman in European clothes and of happy demeanour came to the door of the mission-house. Her face seemed familiar to Mrs. Forsyth. It was Raqula, converted, clothed, and in her right mind. She had come back with her husband and little son to reside in Xolobe, and soon entered the candidates' class, a humble and industrious disciple. She became a member and was regularly married in Xolobe Church, and brought two children to be baptized.

Kate's eldest sister Jane had also gone to school. A quiet diligent plodder, she was soon able to read the New Testament, and the beauty of the life portrayed there won her heart. Casting about in her mind how to procure clothes, she collected bundles of wood which she sold to Mrs. Forsyth. She had nearly amassed sufficient when her father got wind of her intention, seized her hard-earned savings, withdrew her from school, and ordered her not even to think about the new customs. She had no alternative but to submit, and she grew up to womanhood a heathen.

After she married, her husband went to work at the mines and met with a serious injury. Jane was afraid he would die, and the teaching she had received from Mrs. Forsyth came back to her mind, and she turned in her trouble to God and was answered according to her faith. Becoming a candidate at another out-station she was baptized along with her children.

The leavening process went on. Another of Taki's wives was moved to renounce her " red " allegiance, but the position was made so hard for her that she recanted.

Raqula's cousin, Nosimanga, was married to an old witch-doctor and was the mother of two intelligent boys. At a prayer-meeting at her home she was brought to Christ and soon learnt to read. Her husband, strangely enough, put no hindrance in her way; he even accompanied her occasionally to church, though he kept to his own fashion of life.

Taki's cruelty increased with these repeated invasions of his heathen peace. A daughter-in-law was won over by Mrs. Forsyth, but her husband remained obdurate. She was determined, however, to bring up

## THE TYRANNY OF TAKI 93

her infant daughter Su-pi as a Christian, and she clothed her in the new way. When her husband died suddenly her friends jeered at her and said she was being punished. They persecuted her and boycotted her but she remained firm. Then Taki took her in hand. One day he caught her on her knees praying for herself, her child, and her heathen friends. Infuriated he snatched up an assegai and threatened to spear her and kill her if she did not recant. She was so alarmed that she ran out of the kraal and fled over the hills. For a whole week she wandered in the direction of her old home with practically nothing to eat, and then fell dead from starvation and over-fatigue.

When the news reached Taki's kraal he despatched a horseman to bring back the child, who was stripped of her clothing and smeared with red clay, and so received into heathenism. By and by, however, she was allowed to go to school and developed into one of the best scholars, won many prizes, and entered the candidates' class.

Another daughter-in-law lost her husband and turned in her sorrow to Christ. Taki threatened her and she went to 'Smoyana, who took up her case and summoned the man to her presence.

"Taki," she said, "do you like your sheep? and count them? Do you know when you lose one or find one? For there was a man who had a hundred sheep and he lost one, and he went after it a long time, and he was wounded while he sought it, and it was found in your kraal when you were not there. And people said, ' Taki will not be willing to give it up to the owner.' But I said, ' I think he will; I shall see him and try.' "

By this time Taki was sitting bolt-upright, his face working, his eyes staring.

"Taki," she continued, " do not be afraid. I am speaking a parable to you. God is the owner of the sheep that was lost. The sheep is your daughter-in-law whom you have forbidden to come to Christ. Will you give her to her lawful owner?"

Somewhat relieved Taki replied sullenly, " I have no power over her soul. I did forbid her before, but now I have nothing to say."

" Well, I would like you to give her leave to attend the meetings and classes and the Sabbath services."

" All right," he muttered. " She can go. But I forbid you to come any more to the kraal."

## THE TYRANNY OF TAKI

Writing Mr. Davidson on some matters 'Smoyana added a postscript :
"*We are going to make a raid on Taki's house in a body on Sabbath without his permission. Pray for us!*"

Taki is still a heathen.

# VII

## THE WITCH-DOCTOR'S FATE

PASSING, one day, a large group of half-naked men sitting imbibing beer she noticed, in the centre, a commanding figure with a head of tangled grey hair from which strings of blue beads hung pendant to the waist.

It was her stoutest opponent, Loqina the witch-doctor. When he saw her he shouted threateningly,

"Go away, you Government spy; we don't want you."

Mrs. Forsyth's Scottish blood rose at this, and she went forward and fearlessly told him what she thought of him and his ways.

Shortly afterwards a native marriage took place with its attendant abominations of drinking and dancing—and worse. It ended with a free fight between the girls of Xolobe and a neighbouring district. Loqina was present during the seven days of the feast and then went stumbling home. "Loqina

## THE WITCH-DOCTOR'S FATE

is taking the wrong road," cried some one who followed him up and found that the old man's excesses had smitten him blind.

He was thereafter a prisoner in his dirty home and was looked after by Nondika, his queer old wife, to whom he rhapsodised about the wars he had been engaged in, the blood he had shed, and the wounds he had received. His lucrative practice fell off and he was reduced to want.

A little kindness from the white woman worked wonders and he began to come to her meetings. The parable of the lost sheep attracted him strangely. "Tell me about the sheep that was lost," he would say again and again, like a child fascinated by some story, and he never tired of listening to it. When he left Mrs. Forsyth's presence he always bent down and kissed her hand.

He grew poorer and more friendless and was forsaken by his relations. His strength failed as well as his sight and he wished Mrs. Forsyth to go and count his sheep which he had left in the care of a neighbour. The sheep had disappeared, and at the last he was only able to give Nondika a shilling. "Buy some clothes," he said, "and go to church." He did not make any profession but died praying.

The old wife discarded her red clay and with a little help procured some clothes and became a faithful attender at the services. Whether the weather was cold or hot, wet or sunny, she was at the station by sunrise. She was finally baptized by Mr. Davidson, but her home life was not happy. Food and house-room were grudgingly bestowed, and she was often taken violently to task for not being able to complete the work allotted to her in the fields. She caught a chill and died one morning at daybreak, with love in her heart for "God and Jesus and little children."

Another instance of the power of the new teaching at this time gave Mrs. Forsyth much satisfaction. Nomonti, the head wife of the former headman, had become more hardened after her husband's imprisonment and pursued her sinful way. Some of her near relatives, however, forsook their red clay and after probation were admitted to the membership of the church. This seemed to startle her out of her complacency. One day whilst Mrs. Forsyth was passing her hut she saw the woman beckoning to her.

"Well, Nomonti," she said kindly, noticing that she hesitated to speak. As she still seemed at a loss how to begin Mrs. Forsyth went on:

## THE WITCH-DOCTOR'S FATE

" And what do you think of your friends accepting Jesus as their Saviour ? "

" Ma," she exclaimed, " I want to receive Him too ! "

On the green grass by the roadside she knelt and surrendered herself, and a month later was baptized.

Becoming weak and frail in body she was not able for rapid travelling and came down to the Mission house on Saturday and remained until Monday in order not to miss the services. She enjoyed the morning and evening worship and the talks with Mrs. Forsyth, and up to the end was happy and cheerful in her faith.

When she died she pled pathetically in prayer that her Heavenly Father might be with her as she went through the dark valley of the shadow. So well beloved had she become that one hundred and fifty "red" men and women paid the last tribute of respect to her.

# VIII

## A NINE-DAYS' WONDER

As the work developed, and possibilities of extension presented themselves, Mrs. Forsyth longed for an assistant who would relieve her of some of her routine duties. Plan as she would, however, she could not make her slender income stretch sufficiently to cover the cost. She talked the matter over with Mr. Davidson, always her wise counsellor, and as his mind had fixed upon Xolobe for her so it turned now to a society in Scotland which, he was sanguine, would provide her the help she required. This was the Greenock Ladies' Association for Promoting Female Education in Kafraria, which had been instituted in 1841 for the purpose of assisting the work at Emgwali Training Institution.

Acting on his advice she wrote to the Committee describing her service and needs, and received an eager and generous response,

## A NINE-DAYS' WONDER 101

the Society agreeing to send her out £20 a year to pay the salary of an assistant.

Thus was initiated a connection which lasted throughout the whole of her sojourn in Kafraria and formed the principal link between her and the homeland. She corresponded with the Secretary, Miss Prentice, and after her death, with her successor Miss Macfarlane. Month by month the lonely missionary related the story of her work and back came the love and sympathy of an understanding Christian heart. These letters from Miss Macfarlane were a perennial source of cheer and encouragement.

In time other members of the Committee got into touch with her and showed her much kindness. As her name and work began to be better known amongst the congregations of the church, money and boxes of goods for distribution to the natives were sent out to her by work parties, Sunday School children, and others. Two cases from the Greenock ladies contained cotton and woollen material, clothes, stationery, toys, and other articles to the value of £75. These gifts were very welcome; she was able to give the children what they required to attend school, to clothe the natives who renounced their blanket, and to assist the people generally in times of economic distress.

For her first assistant 'Smoyana chose Ntintille, who happened to be a protégée of the Ladies' Association, having been trained at Emgwali. She proved helpful both in school and in visitation, but the climate proved too cold for her constitution and she resigned.

She was succeeded by Bekiwe, her old scholar at Paterson, who, at the instance of Mrs. Macfarlane, of Glasgow, had obtained some training at Emgwali, and was as consistent in her life and as eager and devoted in her service for Christ as ever. She was a nine-days' wonder. The people were amazed to know that this trim, wholesome girl had, been a " red clay " like themselves; but they were also ready to ridicule and intimidate her. She, however, was a thoroughgoing Christian, fearlessly facing their scorn, and denouncing the evils of their heathen customs.

Another subsequent assistant was Antyi Mbanga, who was descended from a royal clan, and was loved and respected by the natives, and exercised real power in the district.

Mrs. Forsyth saw that women like these

A TYPICAL FINGO

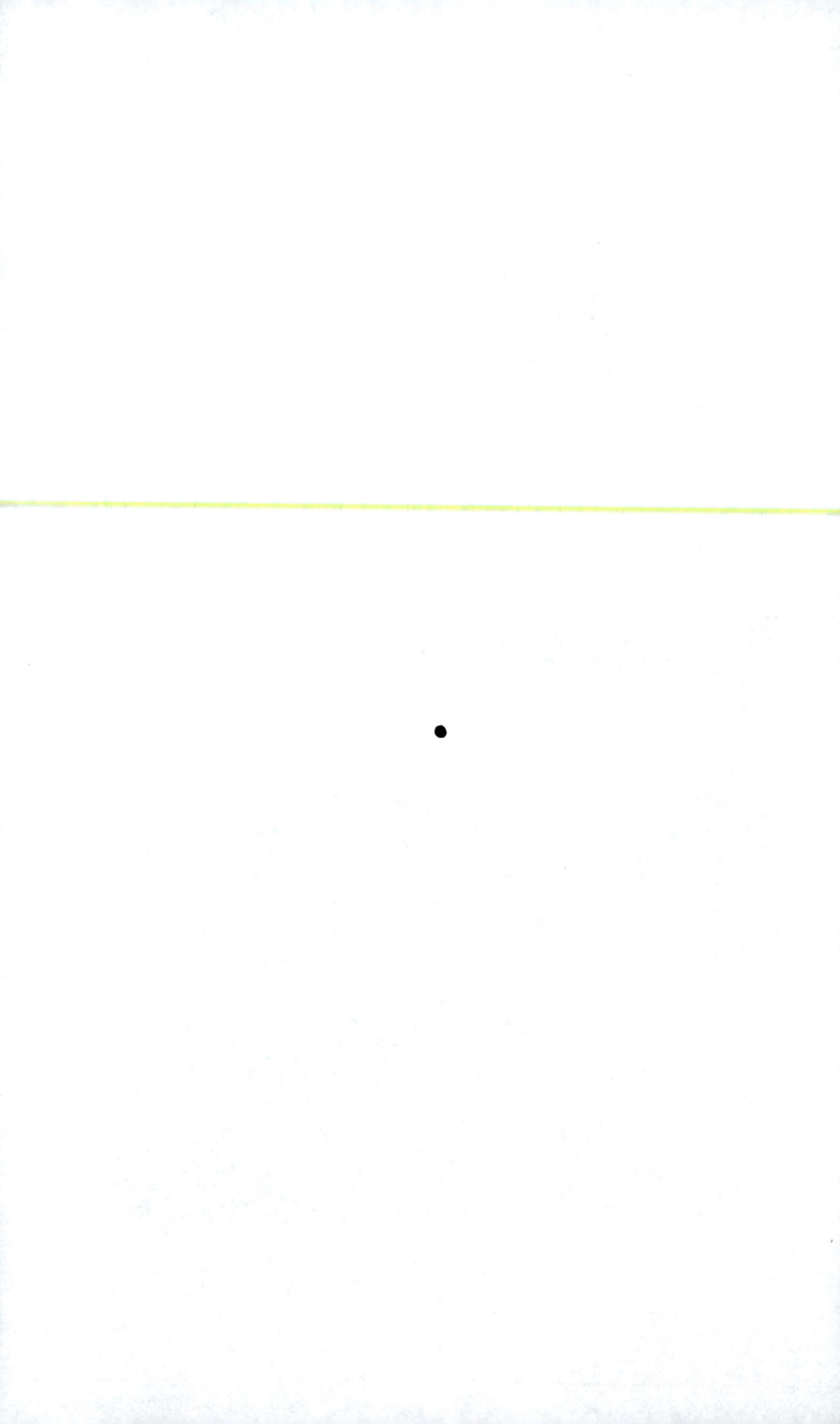

were the hope of Africa. There might, no doubt, be failures, but the example and influence of those who succeeded were beyond all calculation. This conviction led very soon to an important development.

## IX

## THE GREENOCK GIFT

So absorbed was Mrs. Forsyth in her work that she had forgotten to care for her own comfort. She was still living in a damp and dark Kafir hut, out of which she was occasionally washed by the rains. But she was as happy as a queen, and never thought of complaining to any one. The fact, however, came to the knowledge of the Greenock ladies, who could not bear to think of her passing her days and nights in so wretched a dwelling. They made judicious inquiries regarding material and costs, and then through the generosity of a few friends the Committee was able to remit to her the sum of £48 for the purpose of building a two-roomed cottage, one room to be entirely her own, the other to be used as a schoolhouse in wet or cold weather.

The news of the gift fell like a benediction on the heart of the solitary woman. She

## THE GREENOCK GIFT 105

was deeply touched by the thoughtfulness and sympathy it evinced and proceeded joyfully to raise her home. Selecting native workmen who had renounced their heathenism she set them to work. Interest and love stimulated their service and by November 1889 the building was ready. She called it " The Greenock Schoolhouse " in recognition of the source of the gift. Thinking it well to make a little function of the opening she invited the magistrate of the district and her *umfundisi*, Mr. Davidson, to be present. Many Christians from Paterson and elsewhere also travelled to the ceremony, and an ox was killed and roasted for their benefit.

The magistrate gave a speech in which he impressed upon the people the value of education and the great things which Mrs. Forsyth was doing for them and their children. He then distributed the prizes to the scholars. " To see," wrote Mr. Davidson, " red heathen in one of the darkest spots of Africa coming up in half-dozens and reading the Bible both in English and their own language correctly, and repeating from memory whole chapters of the New Testament and Psalms without a mistake, was really marvellous."

Now that there was a regular mission-house, though a humble one, and a proper home atmosphere, Mrs. Forsyth decided to try the experiment of taking in a scholar to live with her. She felt that the chief influence against the redemption of the children was the evil surroundings of their huts, and it might be possible to train up one or two who would grow up into womanhood uncontaminated by heathen scenes and customs and become teachers and inspirers of their race.

The Greenock Society, happy to share the privilege of this development, hastened to offer £10 per annum to cover the cost.

The girl chosen was " Bella Moir," a lovable, affectionate girl, and a good scholar. She proved worthy of the care which 'Smoyana bestowed upon her, bringing many recruits to the school, and exercising a wholesome influence upon all.

" When did you begin to love your Saviour, Bella ? " inquired Mrs. Forsyth one day.

" Only after I came here," she said.

Bella's case was so encouraging that three other children were taken in. Theodore, seven years old, was the son of Matole, the new headman, who voluntarily gave him up to the care of 'Smoyana. She looked forward to the boy becoming a Christian chief and exercising a wide influence for good. To her sorrow he was suddenly withdrawn.

## THE GREENOCK GIFT 107

When she visited his hut she was greatly affected by his shame as he stood before her decked in his blanket and beads. He kept thereafter out of her sight but once she saw him outside the kraal.

" Theodore, do you still pray ? " she asked.

He hung his head. " No, 'Smoyana. My mother forbids me."

Celani was a girl of heathen parents whom Mrs. Forsyth picked up at a kraal down the valley. Whilst speaking to the father the child began to cry, and on the father asking what was the matter she sobbed, " I want to go with the missionary : I want to go to heaven: I don't want to go to hell." To Mrs. Forsyth's surprise the father gave the girl up to her and she became a boarder. Gentle and likeable, she was apt at learning Scripture and was first in examination at repeating long passages from memory.

One day, noticing a troubled look in her face, Mrs. Forsyth asked her what was wrong and learnt that the girl dreaded being taken away. The blow fell soon after. For some unknown reason she was removed, protesting and in tears, and when Mrs. Forsyth went to her hut she was cut to the heart by the expression of sorrow and despair on her face. A year later an epidemic of smallpox swept over the district, and Celani, much disfigured by the disease and suffering from a racking cough, appeared again and was taken into the shelter of the schoolhouse. But after passing the Third Standard and being baptized she left and put on red clay.

The other child, Ida, was only four years when she became a member of the household. Her mother was a superior woman, one of the finest of the converts, but was married to a " red " who neither sympathised with her nor countenanced her ways. Ida was a winsome little thing who was in danger of being spoiled, but under the housemother's careful guidance she grew up into a sweet and clever girl. Mrs. Forsyth wrote of her : " Ida has learned quickly and surpasses all the children of her age at the school. She can read Kafir, spell a little, do simple addition, repeat the multiplication table, and is second best at Bible knowledge." When she was older a woman who promised to take her down to the Communion at Paterson drew back at the last moment. Praying before going to bed Ida said, " We have been disappointed to-day, but we remember what Jesus said upon the Cross, ' Father, forgive them, for they know not what they do.' "

# X

## OFFICIAL TRIBUTES

IT is the good custom of the Church in Scotland to send out delegates at intervals to its various mission-fields, to survey the work being done at the stations, cheer and help the workers, and bring back an account of what they have seen in order to stimulate interest at home. In 1892 Mrs. Forsyth heard that two delegates from the United Presbyterian Board were on their way to Kafraria, the Rev. James Buchanan, the Foreign Mission Secretary, and his son, Mr. J. C. Buchanan, M.A., but scarcely anticipated that they would take the trouble of penetrating to Xolobe.

Mr. Davidson, however, was resolved that she should be seen in her mountain fastness, and there came a day of pleasurable excitement when the cavalcade rode up. Mr. Buchanan was a man of critical discernment and not readily moved, but he was profoundly impressed by Mrs. Forsyth and her work, and both in his official report to the Board and in the magazines of the Church he dwelt upon the remarkable service she was rendering in her " green spot in the desert." In the narrative of his travels over 1910 miles of country he writes :

" As we approached Xolobe we discovered two buildings, one apparently a wattle-and-daub structure with thatched roof; the other, a neat-looking cottage building covered with corrugated iron. . . . Mrs. Forsyth is an unsalaried agent of the mission who has been doing work in this valley for the past seven. years. The tribe among whom she lives and labours are perhaps the rudest and roughest of the native people—a stranger tribe who came from a distance and settled in this valley some years ago. Mrs. Forsyth was at first looked upon by them with considerable suspicion, and her friends were of opinion that she was exposed to many risks in such a community. But by her patient labour, by her kindly interest in the people, both old and young, and by her calm, unfaltering, unflinching courage, she has won her way to their hearts, and exercises a marvellous influence over them. They look upon her as in a very special

## OFFICIAL TRIBUTES

sense their own, and woe betide any one who would attempt to insult or injure her.

" She visits the people in their huts, and gathers them together for worship in the little church. She has some sixty children at her school, whom she teaches to read and to commit to memory portions of Scripture and hymns. She has had about one hundred and seventy young people under her hands, and such a blessing has attended her efforts on their behalf that no fewer than forty of these have been led to profess their faith in Christ, most of whom, after being thoroughly tested by Mr. Davidson's session, have been admitted to the fellowship of the church.

" As we observed Mrs. Forsyth busy at her work; as we thought of the difficulties she had overcome, and the position she had made for herself amongst that barbarous tribe; as we thought of her there single-handed and alone doing the Master's work, supporting herself out of her own resources; as we marked the quiet, genuine happiness that she has in her work, and her humble trustful dependence upon Him whom she loves and serves, we could not refrain from saying that we had witnessed in that valley perhaps the most remarkable sight that had met our eyes throughout all our journeyings.

"There are here many of the elements of the truest heroism. The story of Mrs. Forsyth's work in Xolobe during these past few years is little known because of her modest and unassuming nature, because she looks upon the work as not done by her, but by Him on whom by a simple but sublime faith she depends; but it is not less a story which may well touch our hearts, and that may·serve as an inspiration and a guide to many who have time and means and culture at their disposal, but who cannot find a sphere in which to serve their Lord, and to benefit and bless their fellows."

To this tribute may be added one from Mr. Newton O. Thompson, who was Resident Magistrate of the district until 1895:
"Mrs. Forsyth had no fears. She kept before her the great work which she had come to carry out, and nothing could turn her aside. Hopeful and courageous, she plodded on in the face of much opposition, and although she fully realised the great difficulties in her way, never doubted, and was always cheerful. I was much impressed with the quiet persistent manner in which she overcame all difficulties and carried on the work without any trouble with the people.

## OFFICIAL TRIBUTES 113

I have no doubt she met with many troubles, but, if so, these were always settled quietly, or with the help and support of the missionary from Mbulu, and I cannot recall any instance in which any complaint was brought to the office. Those who at first were doubtful as to the wisdom of the step taken by Mrs. Forsyth came round in the end. Her self-sacrifice and devotion to the work so impressed people (white and black) that all were ready to acknowledge her strength of character and sincerity."

# XI

# AN EXPERIMENT WHICH FAILED

THERE were few busier women in Africa at this time than Mrs. Forsyth. Her days were occupied early and late with a multitude of duties in the interests of the people and her household. Here is a note she gave the Greenock ladies of her activities for one week :

" Prayer-meetings on Monday, Tuesday, and Thursday mornings at daybreak ; meetings on Tuesday and Thursday afternoons ; sewing twice a week before school and visiting afterwards ; plastering outside and inside ; whitewashing ; scrubbing and oiling the stained floors ; baking for Christmas ; killing sheep ; roasting and grinding coffee ; attending to numerous callers."

Sometimes she would leave her routine work and spend a week visiting the more remote kraals. In her eagerness to help and save the people she never thought of herself ;

## AN EXPERIMENT WHICH FAILED

she slept where she could, and ate what native food she could procure, and trudged over the rocky hills indifferent to fatigue and exhaustion.

There came times when, overwhelmed by work and difficulties, she would stand in rueful perplexity and wonder at herself. " I don't suppose any one else would remain here for any length of time," she confessed. There was always some trouble or distress disturbing the order of life. Now it would be a severe drought, now a plague of locusts, now an epidemic of rinderpest amongst the cattle, now a visitation of smallpox or other disease. At these periods every one turned to her for her advice and help and comfort. During one winter, with the assistance of friends in Scotland, she fed forty children daily.

She found at last that she could not compass all her tasks with any degree of satisfaction. " If only I had a white helper," she sighed. The Greenock ladies were always so interested in her work that she made up her mind to lay the situation before them. " Perhaps," she thought, " there may be found at home some lady of consecrated life who may be willing to come out and devote herself and her means to such a service." She ventured to broach the subjcet, and asked the ladies to try and find such an individual. " Give us," she said, " some one filled with the Divine compassion for souls that animated our Saviour."

The suggestion fell on sympathetic hearts; it awakened, indeed, something like enthusiasm. There was only one doubt expressed. Mrs. Forsyth, it was said, was an exception to all rule. " She is one in a thousand and does work that no one else would attempt. But might there not be a risk in asking another to share her trials and privations ? " The risk was, nevertheless, accepted; the ladies determined to go forward in faith.

A Committee was appointed to make known the need, but the effect of the appeal was disappointing. Not one could be found to sacrifice her home life and interests for service amongst the kraals of Kafirland. The Committee met again and again without result. It was not to be baffled. If no one would go as a voluntary worker, perhaps a salary would be an inducement. One friend after another said she would feel it an honour to be allowed to contribute to such a cause, and guaranteed amounts for five years. The total sum raised was beyond all expectation.

## AN EXPERIMENT WHICH FAILED

The choice of the Committee fell upon Miss Isabella Lamb, who was dedicated to the work at a meeting in Greenock at which two South African missionaries, Dr. and Mrs. Soga, were present. The former—a son of the famous Tiyo Soga—advised her to acquire some knowledge of dispensing, and she went for a time to an institution in Edinburgh, where she was taught how to treat simple ailments. In June 1893 she sailed with the Sogas for South Africa.

From East London she covered the same ground as Mrs. Forsyth had done. She was so fatigued by the rough experience that Mrs. Davidson kept her at Paterson for a time to recruit. On arriving at her destination she wrote: " I can't describe the wagon journey, but I don't think I will leave Xolobe until there is a railway."

Mr. Davidson formally introduced her to the people. To the headman he said: " I hope you will receive her kindly and take care of her, along with Mrs. Forsyth."

" Umfundisi," the headman replied, " we know 'Smoyana. She is an old woman and a woman of sense, but she goes to the huts and over the rocks in the night-time. If she does that what will Miss Lamb not do? —for she is young and perhaps flighty. We will take care of them but will not be responsible for them after the sun is down and our people are drinking beer. If they go to a hut and the way is long they must stay till sunrise, or get some one to see them safely home. We receive Miss Lamb."

Then up spoke the headman from Paterson, a Christian, with a deeper knowledge of the forces behind Mrs. Forsyth:

" 'Smoyana is safe. I have seen her come to a flooded river which she was afraid to cross. What does she do? For a minute she puts her hands like this [covering his eyes as if in prayer], then goes bravely over."

Miss Lamb began with all the buoyancy and energy of a newcomer, visited the huts, and with her medicine-chest beside her held continuous levees. Mrs. Forsyth, she declared, was " nice and kind and a thoroughly good Christian." The missionary watched her with shrewd eyes, and wrote that the Committee must not expect too much of her for a year at least, and that it would depend on the care she took of herself during that time what her future in Africa would be. Mrs. Davidson felt very sorry for her. " The work is trying at the best," she said, " and the isolation will be hard on a young person."

## AN EXPERIMENT WHICH FAILED

As the days passed the rose-colours faded out of the life, and difficulties seemed to increase, though they were the ordinary difficulties of a mission-station, which always require courage and patience and faith. The people were hard-hearted. An epidemic of smallpox and measles broke out, and the school had to be closed and visitation given up. The church was burned down. The heat was severe and told on her health. Despite an occasional visit to Paterson, where she was mothered by Mrs. Davidson, she began to suffer from depression of spirits, sleeplessness, and lack of appetite. She brooded over the fact that she had undertaken duties for which she had not the physical strength. Finally the District Surgeon reported that she was suffering from anaemia and recommended that she should be removed to some place where the climate was more bracing, the surroundings more congenial, and the duties lighter.

The Ladies' Committee at home met immediately this report was received and sent out a kind message to the effect that she might feel happier if she knew she was not bound to stay but was free to do as she wished, and that if she thought it best to resign they would pay her passage back.

She resigned but remained in South Africa, finding more suitable employment as a nurse in a hospital at Queenstown.

Thus ended Mrs. Forsyth's dream of a helper and companion from the homeland. She never sought another, but continued in her isolation and loneliness, with only an occasional visit from a missionary to keep her in touch with white civilisation. She had a profound belief that she would obtain all the strength and support she needed.

The episode is like a flash of light in the darkness, revealing the exceptional character of the conditions amidst which she lived, and proving that not all would-be missionaries are fitted for the rough and lonely work of pioneering in Africa. "Few women," writes the Rev. John Lundie of Malan Mission, "have the nerve for such work. Fewer still can stand the isolation and the disappointments with native character without breaking down in health and spirits. Mrs. Forsyth always seemed to me fitted by nature, temperament, and physique, as well as spiritually, for the niche she filled."

# XII

## A FIRE AND A REVIVAL

THE old wattle-and-daub building in which services were held had begun to leak and Mrs. Forsyth set about re-thatching it. It was the hot season. Over a hundred women carried the grass, and a squad of men cut and prepared the saplings for the verandah poles. All was finished, and the thatcher was burning the discarded material when the wind arose and carried a spark to the new roof. It blazed up like tinder and in a trice the entire building was consumed.

Looking at the little heap of ashes Mrs. Forsyth said to those around : " There is only one thing to do ; we must build another." That is the characteristic spirit of African missionaries when confronted by disaster ; they never acknowledge defeat or give way to despair. They simply begin again. Life in the wilds, indeed, is but a series of beginnings.

The services, meanwhile, were held in the schoolroom which was crowded to excess by both Christians and "reds" so that the children had to find a place under the table. There was no one more relieved than the missionary when the new building was completed. The opening was a red-letter event in the history of Xolobe. Along with the magistrate and Mr. Davidson there was present Mr. Candlish Koti, who had been appointed assistant at Paterson. A native evangelist of promise, he had been sent to Scotland as a deputy to the Jubilee Synod of the United Presbyterian Church and had just returned. "I feel," he said, "as if I had had a tremendous dream. When I tell people about things I have seen they seem to be listening to one who is relating a dream, and are quite unable to realise what you tell them."

The building cost £50, the greater part of which the people themselves contributed. At the opening service they gave £9, mostly in small sums, such as tickies (threepenny pieces) and pennies, and in stock, such as sheep and goats and fowls. One heathen man laid down 10s. with the remark, "My cattle are dead, and there is no harvest, I can't afford any more." After the service

# A FIRE AND A REVIVAL 123

the company adjourned to the open where they feasted and then quietly dispersed at sunset to their homes.

The event seemed to shake the people out of their routine and stir their deeper feelings, for it was followed by a movement amongst women and children which was akin to revival. The church was packed on every occasion. One woman walked with her baby strapped to her back a difficult mountain journey of three hours to be present at the services. "It is true," remarked 'Smoyana, "that love lends wings to the feet."

Special meetings were also held in the surrounding huts which sometimes went on all night. "We used to come here as red heathen to dance," said one woman to Mrs. Forsyth, "now we come to pray." A notable part was taken by the women themselves who were singularly eloquent and fervent in their prayers. One, who was old and poor, poured forth her soul thus:

"Lord, I have no home. Thou art my home. I have no goods. Thou art my portion. I have no food. Thou art the bread which came down from heaven, of which if we eat we shall never hunger or thirst."

Mrs. Forsyth was happy. "My cup runneth over," she exclaimed again and again, and she attributed all to prayer put up on her behalf in Scotland. Her vision expanded. She not only wanted "Xolobe for Christ." Her motto now was "Africa for Christ." She urged her friends to wider prayer.

# XIII

## THE MIRACLE OF TEN YEARS

WHAT impact had this one lonely worker made on the massed heathenism of Xolobe during her first ten years of service ?
In her humility she was only conscious of how little had been achieved, and yet she had accomplished a result which onlookers considered little short of marvellous. Her sole instruments had been a simple gospel ministry, absolute faith, and indomitable tenacity of purpose. With these she had created, out of the crudest heathenism, a civilised and Christian community. There had been 117 baptisms and admissions to the worship of the church, and many candidates were ready and fit for joining. She had established a series of religious organisations exercising an ever-increasing influence. The day school she had started was now an important institution, the work of which was rapidly expanding beyond the limit of her

powers. The people who had opposed her and resisted her ministrations were at last friendly; she was looked upon as a mother to them all, their trusted adviser, helper, and guide. She could go alone to any kraal, night or day, even when a beer drink was in progress, and feel that she was respected and safe.

It was, indeed, a miracle of patient toil and persistence. For one has to bear in mind the untold expenditure of thought, prayer, and energy which each changed life represented. Sometimes she was years shepherding some wild heart. There was one heathen kraal which she had visited continuously since she arrived without observing the least sign of change, yet she never lost confidence. In the tenth year one of the women inmates came forward and surrendered herself, and the missionary welcomed her with humble gratitude. It was such incidents that kept her life flushed with hope and gave her the joy which made her work endurable and glad.

Perhaps nothing thrilled her so much as when she heard that the dying had passed away in Christian faith and assurance. A young married woman, one of her original scholars, lay on her death-bed. " My body

## THE MIRACLE OF TEN YEARS 127

is weak," she murmured, "but my soul is in perfect peace." Her first convert, a young man, while dying, kept his New Testament lovingly clasped in his hand. Afterwards it was removed and given to Mrs. Forsyth, who sent it to the ladies in Greenock as a pathetic, yet significant, symbol of the dawning of the new era in Xolobe.

Not that all the dark features of heathenism had been eradicated, or that all hostility to her teaching had ceased. There were times when even her extraordinary courage and hopefulness faltered and her spirits drooped. At some of the meetings only a few would appear. The others would be away at a beer-drinking. Superstition was still rife. Scholars would be withdrawn from the school because 'Smoyana had sent the rinderpest amongst them to destroy their cattle!

There were men and women, too, with whom she could do nothing, and her grief would have been unmitigable had she not remembered that even her Master, with all His power, could work no change with some people because of their unbelief. Many were sympathetic towards her but shy of her message. It was almost ludicrous to watch their attitude. They shunned the church when services were going on and yet were eager enough to help her in any work that had to be done to the building. Others desired to come and hear her, drawn by a powerful curiosity as to that Unknown God of hers, and they would squat outside, longing, yet afraid, to enter, lest they might be converted.

There were troubles also with her own members and bravely did she meet them. " A few Sabbaths ago," she writes, " it was my painful duty to warn the Christian people amongst us not to give their sons to the heathen custom of circumcision, and its attendant evils. This custom permeates all classes, Christian and heathen, and yearly it is the beginning of a downward course to many, who are thus lost to God and to purity of life. I could see that my audience were not in sympathy with me. The native evangelist held down his head, and wiped the perspiration from his forehead. Perhaps the sins of his youth were rising before him. 2 Corinthians vi. 17, 18 were my last words to them, ' Wherefore, come out from among them, and be ye separate, saith the Lord, and touch not the unclean thing ; and I will receive you, and will be a Father unto you, and ye shall be my sons and daughters, saith the Lord Almighty.' The native evangelist proceeded with his work afterwards, making no allusion to what had gone before."

But the rank swamp of heathenism had been cleared of its worst elements, and although at times whiffs of moral miasma drifted chokingly over the district the atmosphere was infinitely purer than it had been when she arrived that summer evening ten years before.

# XIV

## ABDICATION

ANOTHER stage in the quiet evolution of the work was reached when the day school passed out of Mrs. Forsyth's hands. Her chief thought was centred there, for she realised that if she secured the youth of the district she would be laying a secure foundation for a Christian future, and she was continually pondering how to increase its usefulness and influence.

When a new magistrate was appointed he was told of her work. " I wish I could do something to help her," he exclaimed. The remark reached her ears and she promptly sent him a message to the effect that the best thing he could do for her was to stir up the " red " people to send their children to school. He thought that would rather increase her toil than lessen it, but he, nevertheless, acceded to her suggestion and held conferences with the headman with excellent

THE GREENOCK SCHOOLHOUSE

HANDING OVER THE SCHOOL TO THE GOVERNMENT TEACHER.

## ABDICATION 131

results for the school. It grew steadily in numbers until sixty-four boys and girls were attending regularly.

The efficiency of the teaching was always tested at Christmas, when the parents and friends of the pupils gathered to witness a display of their powers. Examinations were conducted in Bible knowledge, and it astonished Mr. Davidson, who usually presided, to learn how thoroughly they had been grounded, and how extensive and intelligent was their acquaintance with the Book. Over 90 per cent of the answers were, as a rule, correct. All the children repeated the Ten Commandments and the Beatitudes, and some could recite whole chapters without a mistake. Hymns were sung without the book and problems in arithmetic solved. There was always one who was proud of being able to say off the multiplication table backwards. Specimens of sewing work were also exhibited. The proceedings ended with the distribution of dolls and toys from a Christmas tree, and the presentation of Bibles to those who had been baptized.

It was little wonder that there began to be talk of having the school properly inspected and of securing Government aid.

Mrs. Forsyth foresaw what that meant—the appointment of a certificated teacher; but with her usual common sense and adaptability she was ready to accept the change for the good of Xolobe.

"It will be a sore wrench to me when it comes," she wrote. "But I must try to get over the feeling by throwing myself heart and soul into the other work." This was calling her with ever more insistent summons. She brooded over the fact that fifty men and women had died in their heathenism during her sojourn amongst them. "Visitation and evangelisation are urgent and I must do more." It was her constant cry.

Shortly afterwards the school was taken over by the Government; and she abdicated in favour of Simon Ndima, a trained teacher, the son of a Paterson headman, who was given Antyi as an assistant. Mrs. Forsyth feared that a Government teacher might not accord due attention to Bible instruction and said so to Simon. He looked at her sorrowfully. "'Smoyana," he replied," I know that no good can be done without that Book."

She was present when he gave his first Bible lesson on the birth of Jesus, and was struck by its simplicity and impressiveness. With relief she wrote to her friends, "I leave the school in his hands without fear." She and Mr. Davidson were appointed joint-managers.

The school continued to flourish and the curriculum was widened, cookery, sewing, and knitting being amongst the subjects added, whilst a qualified assistant replaced Antyi who devoted herself to evangelistic work. It was always a grief to the teacher that the older pupils left so soon, their places being taken by the little ones, but Mrs. Forsyth wisely said, " I am quite pleased to see the dear wee things coming from heathen kraals to be taught. God's standards are different from man's."

The teacher at this time lost his own little child, and, sorrowing over the event as if the infant had been her own, Mrs. Forsyth went over with material for the burial. Two women sewed a white gown and cap, and the child was placed in a rough coffin covered with black muslin. Amidst the weeping of those present, Christian and heathen, one of the elders spoke a few words from the passage, " Now is Christ risen from the dead " ; and then the old grandfather took the coffin in his arms and proceeded to the grave, where he prayed with such emotion that he completely broke down.

## XV

## THE DOCTOR'S WARNING

RELIEVED from the duties of the school Mrs. Forsyth gave herself more completely to the general work of the station, organising it on more comprehensive lines, and adding new agencies as she saw need.

All this activity she carried on unaided save by her native assistant and one or two voluntary workers. "It is amazing the work she accomplishes," Mr. Davidson reported in 1902. She held the usual Sunday services, a candidates' class, a junior candidates' class, which met on Monday morning and was attended by over sixty boys and girls—a Sunday School with a senior class for women who were learning to read the Bible, and prayer-meetings both in the church and the huts. Not content with these stated events she gathered all the school girls and lads of the church on Saturdays and dealt with each apart.

## THE DOCTOR'S WARNING

She also began a branch of the Upward and Onward Society which met on Sunday and was well attended. The membership of the Society throughout the district of Mbulu and out-stations was over five hundred. In this connection she came into touch with the Countess of Aberdeen. To commemorate the twenty-fifth anniversary of the Society the latter sent out a gift of pale-blue satin bookmarks, and Mrs. Forsyth was amused to find at a local ceremony that the women had adorned their bodies with them. The Society later became incorporated with the Women's Christian Association of the Presbyterian Church of South Africa.

Meetings to pray for rain were a special feature of the work. In this northern storm-lashed land of ours such gatherings seem strange, but droughts in South Africa are of frequent occurrence. When the sun shone pitilessly for weeks on a slowly shrivelling land, the people turned to their "rain-makers" to break the spell. Mrs. Forsyth endeavoured to raise their materialistic conception to a higher and more spiritual plane. To her meetings the heathen came in large numbers, the church never being able to hold them all. Her attitude was a humble waiting upon God, maker of heaven and earth, and she was justified in a wonderful way. Here is a single instance told in her own words. " In consequence of the lack of the summer rain the corn and maize were stunted and drooping. The heathen headman sent a request for special prayer to be made. On the very day the prayer was offered the rain began to fall. As they continued to pray it fell in torrents and their crops were saved." Over and over again in her reports comes the laconic sentence, " We prayed for rain; our prayers were answered." The people declared that it was she who had brought the rain, but " of course," she said, " it was God."

She was giving much thought and time to the training of her boarders, whom she wished to be an object-lesson to the people. Usually she had from four to seven under her care, for each of whom the Greenock ladies contributed £5 per annum. She gave them good plain food and clothing, kept them busy during working hours, but allowed them plenty of leisure for recreation and play, and if they needed correction she did not spare them. As a result they were seldom ill, and were a contented, merry little company.

Ida was still one of the number and was as

## THE DOCTOR'S WARNING

bright and diligent as ever. Seemingly without effort she always came to the front, and was first in general intelligence. She was eager to continue her education and become an evangelist to her own people. Young as she was she was already beginning to speak to them of her knowledge of the peace and joy that attended the Christian life. So bright and promising was her character that when she could advance no higher in the school the Greenock Committee decided to send her to Emgwali Institution for the training she desired. There she also proved an apt and painstaking pupil, adding to her acquirements a thorough knowledge of sewing and baking. " I am glad you taught me to be a Christian child," she wrote to Mrs. Forsyth. " I want you to forgive me for all the unkind things I did to make you sorry. I am asking God to forgive me and trying hard to do my duty."

Another boarder was Eliza, who was clever both at housework and lessons. She was the niece of the headman, and ultimately left to become cook to a white family. All the others did well, and one stood highest in the Presbyterial examination.

Such incessant toil at her age—she was now fifty-eight—told upon Mrs. Forsyth's health, and there was a lowering of vitality which made her a ready victim to influenza. The attack was a severe one, and she was in bed for many weeks. When at Paterson attending the marriage of Mr. Davidson's daughter she saw Dr. Arnot — who had married the other daughter—and he examined her thoroughly and gave his verdict.

"There is no organic disease," he said; "but the muscles of your heart are strained. You must not take any more long walks to heathen kraals. If you insist on doing that you will simply drop down some day—sooner than later."

Her comment on this to a friend in Scotland was: "I am beginning to feel that I am in the sere and yellow leaf. We are both nearing the borderland, and the only thing that grieves me is the number of opportunities for serving our dear Lord and Saviour I have missed. What an unprofitable servant I have been! I would like you to know that when my time comes I would not like a single word to be written about me but this:

> Not in mine innocence I trust,
> I bow before Thee in the dust,
> And through my Saviour's blood alone
> I look for mercy at Thy throne."

# XVI

## VISITORS FROM SCOTLAND

THE union of the United Presbyterian Church, with which she was connected, and the Free Church left her position unaffected. She had been appointed an honorary worker by the Foreign Mission Board of the Church, and did not come, like other ladies on the foreign staff, under the jurisdiction of the new Women's Foreign Mission Committee of the united Church. But, like many another missionary, she was less of a personality than ever. She was now one of the most obscure units in the vast missionary force of the united body, occupying a remote and solitary outpost, and she pursued her tranquil way unknown to all save an interested and loyal few. Only an infrequent notice about her work appeared in the *Missionary Record* of the Church. " It is seldom," wrote Dr. Robson, the Editor, on one occasion, " that we can say anything about her quiet but splendid ministry of service." When Dr. Robson died, she, like all the missionaries, missed his friendly interest. " He was like a father to us all," she said, " so great intellectually and spiritually and withal as humble as a child."

She was greatly cheered and strengthened by a passing glimpse of two visitors from the homeland, distinguished members of her former church, and prominent workers in the united body, Mr. and Mrs. Duncan M'Laren of Edinburgh, well known for their deep and generous interest in missions and missionaries. As Mrs. M'Laren edited the *Women's Missionary Magazine* of the Church she was specially sympathetic to the women's side of the work, and was anxious, while in South Africa, to see Xolobe and Mrs. Forsyth. Both visitors came away impressed by the saintliness of her character, her absolute trust upon God, and her devotion to the work. Here is Mrs. M'Laren's own account of her experience :

" Mrs. Forsyth had come over the mountains from Xolobe to meet us at Paterson. We thought it best after a short rest to accompany her on her return home. The first hill we had to surmount was like a stony staircase. The road leading over it

# VISITORS FROM SCOTLAND 141

was so steep, so bad, so impossible for horses, that Mr. Davidson kindly gave us four oxen to draw our cart and us up. After a time our horses were inspanned, and by walking up the hills we managed to drive the greater part of the way. Eventually we left our cart at a kraal, and walked, amid grand and wild surroundings, to the little Mission-house, perched on a ridge, with a rocky drift in front and a deep dark cañon behind.

" For long Mrs. Forsyth lived in a Kafir hut, but owing to the strong wishes of her friends she consented to the little Mission-house being built. It had only one good room, the other two, which opened off this middle one at each end, being very small. True to her constant practice that God and His work must come first, Mrs. Forsyth had given up her one bright room entirely as a class-room, the mud-and-wattle schoolroom close by being quite inadequate to contain the children who come to be taught. The two little rooms she had for herself were bare and destitute even of very ordinary comforts, but her six little native maidens, who lived with her, and whom she was training for God, kept them scrupulously clean and tidy. There was not even a garden round the Mission-house, because, not being properly enclosed, the pigs ate up everything she tried to grow.

"The church, a simple structure, was close by. It, too, was lacking in sufficient accommodation for the people who attended.

"One of the Christians we saw interested us very much, a bright girl of thirteen. This child, after she had confessed in the heathen kraal that she loved Jesus and meant to serve Him, was chased out of the kraal and over the ridges by her father, whip in hand. She took refuge in the Mission-house, and after a time the wrath of the father so abated that she was allowed to go home.

"I shall always be glad that I heard Mrs. Forsyth pour out her heart in prayer to God in the Kafir tongue. I could not understand or follow the petitions, but I shall never forget the nearness of the Divine presence in that little room, or the shining face of His devoted messenger as we rose from our knees.

"In the morning the Christians had met to pray for rain, and shortly after a thunderstorm broke. Rain was still falling heavily as we started again to traverse the ten miles of wilderness lying between Xolobe and Mbulu. Dark clouds made the deep chasms look deeper still, and added a grandeur to

## VISITORS FROM SCOTLAND 143

the wild rocky heights, but away in the west was a gleam of wonderful light. It seemed as we looked the picturing forth of the blessing that was surely coming to dark Xolobe."

Mrs. Forsyth was equally impressed by Mrs. M'Laren, and wrote of her as possessing a " wonderful personality." The correspondence which followed the visit was a source of help and comfort to the solitary missionary, and the extracts from her letters which Mrs. M'Laren inserted in the *Women's Missionary Magazine* made her known to a wider circle.

The ecclesiastical crisis which occurred a few years later made no difference in South Africa, all the missionaries adhering to the United Free Church. " I hope," Mrs. Forsyth wrote, " no one at home will be unduly troubled by what has happened. God will provide for the Church both at home and abroad. How often have we experienced that God is able to make all things work together for good to those who love Him."

## XVII

## A BIGGER HOUSE OF GOD

IN 1905 the Greenock ladies arrived at the conclusion that the usefulness of their Association had reached its limit. The natives whom they had been assisting were now sensible of the advantage of higher education and willing to pay for it, and it was felt that they should be left to their own resources. With this decision the missionaries on the spot agreed; the time had come, they thought, when the principle of self-support should be put into operation. Mrs. Forsyth remarked that she was still quite able for the work of training the boarders, and there was never any lack of applicants, but the need was not so pressing and few required help. She added, " Your Society has done good work in Africa for God, and what it has done for me will be held in everlasting remembrance. Greenock Schoolhouse and the churches and the children you have

## A BIGGER HOUSE OF GOD 145

helped will not be forgotten here or before God."

Ida was then home from Emgwali for the holidays, a bright capable girl of exceptional promise, and Mrs. Forsyth, looking upon her, was moved to ask the Association, before disbanding, to make provision for completing her education and enabling her to carry out her desire to become a teacher. This was readily agreed to and a sum was laid aside for the purpose. Ida gained a good conduct certificate, passed out successfully, and obtained an assistantship first at Mbulu and then in a Wesleyan School.

After sixty-four years of faithful and successful service the Society dissolved, to live again, however, in an informal way; for the ladies could not bear to break the tie with Mrs. Forsyth so suddenly, and they continued to take an interest in her doings and to support a native assistant for the purpose of living with her and attending to her needs.

Mrs. Forsyth, accordingly, went on with her practice of sending the ladies regular reports regarding the progress of the work. The character of these may be gathered from the heading she always placed upon them—" The Lord's Work." There was never anything in them about *her* service. As one of her correspondents remarked, "She never wrote much about herself; it was her work that stood first with her." She very seldom used the personal pronoun, preferring the word "we." Her reports were records of the personal history of her people, accounts of individual awakening and conversions, or relapse and restoration, of baptisms and marriages, and narrations of the trials, sorrows, and temptations of the women and girls. So simple and uneventful was the story they told that she expressed the hope the ladies would not find them too "dreich." When missionaries who knew her were informed of these reports they said: "Mrs. Forsyth will never give you any real idea of her work or its results. She would not do so if you saw her face to face."

It was not long before the ladies had the opportunity of giving practical expression to their interest. The church, used also as the day school, was becoming too small for its purposes. There were over fifty members in full communion, and the congregation felt the discomforts of overcrowding. "Can we not have a bigger House of God?" they asked.

MARRIED WOMEN OUTSIDE THEIR HUT.

## A BIGGER HOUSE OF GOD 147

The matter was talked of but there had been a succession of bad seasons and poverty was widespread, and nothing was done. Then action was hastened by a threat from the Government Inspector. "The school is becoming too cramped," he said, "I must close it if better accommodation is not provided." This was not to be thought of. There was an attendance of over eighty and the school was second best in the district. Mrs. Forsyth and Mr. Davidson laid their heads together and planned an ambitious scheme. They would build a substantial brick church with stone foundations, iron pillars, and verandah, which would cost about £500 and be worthy of the Master's cause. The elders, headman, and counsellors heartily supported the idea. Where the money was to come from neither the *umfundisi* nor the White Mother knew, but they had the simple faith which moves mountains.

Mr. Davidson came up and called a meeting to start the movement, but that day all the heathen population were at a dance, the culmination of a two-months' bout of immorality, and only the Christians appeared. Still, when the preliminary gifts were gathered in—£12 : 11s. in money, 11 sheep, 6 goats, 1 heifer, and 1½ bags of grain—it was remarkable that the largest donations came from the " red " inhabitants who also offered free labour to quarry the stone and bring the material from a station two days' journey away.

When the Greenock ladies heard of the project they hastened to send their aid. A first instalment of £100 was sent out and lodged in the bank, and Mrs. Forsyth proceeded with the arrangements. It was a task which proved one of the most trying and harassing she had ever ventured upon. Drought came and weakened the oxen to such an extent that they were unable to draw the material and many died. The gang of native workmen were lazy and incompetent, requiring the firm management which she was too gentle and forbearing to exercise. The brickmakers forsook their work and others broke their promises. Mr. Davidson had now retired at the age of seventy-six after forty years' service and she was without ministerial guidance and support, but she went bravely on fighting her difficulties.

It was, however, with profound relief that she welcomed a new face on the scene. This was the Rev. George S. Stewart who had come out from Scotland to be minister

## A BIGGER HOUSE OF GOD 149

at Emgwali. He was one who could appreciate the noble work going on at Xolobe, and he rode over occasionally to see Mrs. Forsyth and became her warm friend and helper. One of the first matters he had to put right had given her much pain. The headman, Matole, had charge of the local contributions for the new building and had embezzled them. Mr. Stewart gave him the option of restoring the funds or being reported at headquarters, and he chose the former course.

The idea of a church entirely of brick was abandoned, and iron, lined with brick, and an inner lining of wood, substituted. From Emgwali Mr. Stewart brought a native carpenter and two other experienced tradesmen and set them to work. It was interesting to Mrs. Forsyth to watch the bearing and industry of these men and note how Christian training influenced the character of their workmanship. Along with the wagon drivers they held worship every evening.

Among those who carried the bricks was a girl whose stunted appearance drew Mr. Stewart's attention. " That is Celani Nopina," said Mrs. Forsyth, " or rather, Nagiwe Nkuhlu is her name now. She used to be one of my best boarders."

It will be remembered that Celani left the school and returned to the mire of heathenism. While in company with a "red" boy on the way to participate in some vile custom a thunderstorm came on and her companion was struck dead by lightning. The incident seemed to impress her but she continued to avoid Mrs. Forsyth. Now, however, a change had come over her; she haunted the Mission-house looking miserable and unhappy, and was given any odd work to do. One day, while she was attending to the garden, Mrs. Forsyth asked her if she remembered the Scripture she had learned in her youth, and she replied that she did, and the missionary was confident that she would win her back.

When completed the church was a simple little building, but the people were as proud of it as a more cultured race would have been of a cathedral. They had contributed £100 towards its erection whilst the friends in Scotland had sent out £200. Mr. Stewart presented a water-tank to remind all of the promise of Christ to those who drank of the living water, and it remains to this day, a memorial of his interest and lovingkindness. "I can never," Mrs. Forsyth says, "be thankful enough for his aid."

# XVIII

## MR. STEWART'S PEN-PICTURE

MR. STEWART was one of the missionaries supported by the children of the United Free Church, and occasionally he sent them a letter which was printed as a leaflet and circulated amongst the Sunday Schools. In one of these he wrote about Mrs. Forsyth and the life she led. The description, in its simplicity and charm, brings Xolobe and its White Mother more vividly before the reader than a more elaborate delineation, and here it is given :

" About forty miles from Emgwali, far over the Great Kei River, there is a beautiful big valley called Xolobe Valley. Along both sides of it are great hills, steep and rocky, with huts dotted along the lower slopes, and woods here and there full of beautiful birds. Near the end of the valley there is a rocky ledge and a precipice with trees growing out of the cracks of the rocks, and on the top of this ledge there is a tiny brick house and a school, with galvanised iron roofs which you can see from miles away glittering in the sun. All along the slopes are many huts, and this one house stands alone.

"If you were to ride there—you could not drive, the road is so steep—you would be met at the door by a kind-looking Scottish lady with very gentle eyes, named Mrs. Forsyth, who would welcome you in heartily. Before you had time to tell who you were she would go away and come back in a minute or two with a cup of tea to refresh you after your long, hot ride. Then you would not be five minutes in the house till you felt that you were very much at home, and that this was an old familiar friend who was talking with you. For you would find this lady make you so welcome, and heap such kindness on you as no mere stranger could do.

"And as you sat and watched, you would see black men and women and boys and girls come in dressed in their red blankets, and all would get a kind word and a welcome, and many who had come from far would get food. And though you could not tell what was being said in the musical Kafir speech, it would be easy for you to tell that this

## MR. STEWART'S PEN-PICTURE 153

lady was much beloved by these half savage folk. Some of the women would have little black babies tied on their backs, with big dancing eyes and such soft velvety skins, and every baby, too, would get a kind word or a loving touch from this gentle lady of that little lonely house in Xolobe Valley.

" When the night came, she would leave her own bed for your comfort, and would sleep on a chair or anywhere, only she would never tell you that; you would need to find it out. But I don't think you would sleep much at night. All the night through you would likely hear, from some of the huts nearer or farther away, great shouting and chanting of strange wild voices, and clapping of hands. You would hear too, on many a night, voices crying out in strife, and the loud rattle of the sticks as the people fought. And you would wonder at a lady living alone, save for two little Kafir girlies, among such wild scenes and sounds. You would be afraid, for often blood is shed, and often men are wounded and sometimes men are killed.

" And if you went visiting among these huts, you would sometimes be afraid too, for after these long nights of drinking and of dancing or of fighting, the men and women are often sulky and cross, and often there are fierce dogs at the huts. Only a short time ago, while this lady was going from hut to hut, trying to tell the people about Christ, a dog sprang out at her and bit her in the face. But nothing will keep her from going.

" And she has long rough ways to walk, steep and stony, and the African sun burns like a flame of fire. A lonely place and a wild people, and hard, hard work. What keeps a lady there ?

"·If you asked this lady why she lived there, she would tell you she loved to live there. And if you still asked ' Why,' she would tell you, as she tells the wild people round, of the great love of God that gave Jesus to us, and of the love that led Him to the Cross. She would tell you of the love that sent Him to seek the lost, over stony ways, and through hunger and thirst and under burning suns. And she would tell you how that love burned in her heart till she felt compelled to rise up and follow Him to the huts and the steep paths of the Xolobe Valley in heathen Africa.

" And she would tell you how she did not feel lonely, for Jesus was her companion on these long, hot paths, and how she was not afraid, for God watched her home through the wild African nights. And she would tell

## MR. STEWART'S PEN-PICTURE

you how she did not shrink from the rude, sulky drunkards, for she loved them, and pitied and wanted to help them.

" And she would tell you how God was working miracles still in that great valley, and turning these dark souls to the brightness of the Lord.

" I want you all to know her and to love her, and to pray for her. She lives such a brave, happy, suffering life, that it will do all you bairns good to know even a little about her. Pray for her sometimes in the bright mornings, as you think of her walking down the steep hill paths in the burning day, to carry Christ's Gospel to those who are glad to hear and to those who turn away. Pray for her as the darkness comes, when you think of her toiling home at night, tired and hungry, while the dark woods mutter and whisper, and the drunken call and the drunken song ring along the valley. Pray for her, as you think of her alone in that wild place, a place often like the dark valley of the shadow. And as you think of her and try to see her, listen as her lips open, and hear her words : ' Yea, though I walk through the valley of the shadow of death, I will fear no evil, for Thou art with me, Thy rod and Thy staff they comfort me.' "

## XIX

## THE NEW UMFUNDISI AND HIS SISTER

THE·Rev. William Auld, M.A., a son of the Rev. James M. Auld of Columba Station, was appointed to succeed Mr. Davidson at Paterson. Born at Emgwali, and educated at Capetown and Glasgow, he was inspired with true missionary zeal. As he was unmarried he brought his sister, Miss Etta M. Auld, to keep house for him. It was a happy circumstance for Mrs. Forsyth. Miss Auld was a warm-hearted capable girl. Both she and her brother had known the missionary from their earliest days; the story of her work was familiar to them, and as they grew up they frequently met her when visiting the Davidsons.

After they settled at Paterson they made it their business to look after her welfare and comfort. Mr. Auld treated her with all the consideration of a son, and would often

## THE NEW UMFUNDISI 157

go up and assist her and adjust knotty points that arose in the course of her work. Miss Auld came more intimately into contact with her, " and," she says, " I learned to love her for her noble life of devotion and self-sacrifice which she did not count a sacrifice but a joy."

The girl often spent days at Xolobe, and the two would take a rug and a couple of cushions and go out and sit at the point where they had the best view of the beautiful valley, and there they would indulge in long talks, and the visitor would hear stories of the missionary's earlier days, of the parents who had died when she was a child, of her brother and sisters, and of episodes, both sombre and glad, in her later career. It was clear to Miss Auld that she had drunk deep of the bitter cup of sorrow, and that she had learnt through suffering to understand and sympathise with and help others.

And then, dismissing her memories, the missionary would accompany the girl down to the stream, and with light heart take off her stockings and shoes and paddle gaily in the water like any child.

With Miss Auld let us walk up to the unpretentious little Mission-house on the hill-top :

" You stepped into what she called the

'schoolroom,' a bare apartment with a table, a couple of forms, and a desk. Here she met with all who came to see her. Here, also, morning and evening prayers were held, as well as the weekly prayer-meeting and the Women's Manyano (Association), whilst on Sunday morning the first early comers were wont to gather in it for a class.

"At the end of this room was a door which opened into her bedroom. It was simply furnished like the rest of the house. There was a single bed, from which if you raised yourself you could command, through the window, a view of the new church and the valley. A packing-case, with a drape over it served as a toilet-table. A small corner bracket, on which stood her travelling clock and a few photos, a small table at the window, a large native basket for soiled linen, a small washstand, and a couple of cabin trunks completed the furnishing of the room.

"Stepping back into the schoolroom you found another door leading into the dining-room, which contained a table, two or three easy-chairs—all old pensioners—a folding bed which often did noble service, and a small table used as a sideboard, above which hung a bookcase with her few well-read and much treasured books.

## THE NEW UMFUNDISI 159

" A door to the left as you entered led into a small pantry, while another with a glass upper half led you on to the verandah where you could always obtain a view of the valley. At the right end of the verandah was the kitchen with a small room attached often occupied by her servant. Along the front verandah ran a rough trellis over which vines were trained, these giving cool shade and abundance of fruit in the season.

" In a small patch of ground, enclosed by a fence of aloes and thorn bush in front of the house and along the side, she cultivated all the vegetables she used and a few fruit trees. A mealie field took up part of the enclosure between the church and the house, but as the soil was stony and of no great depth she never reaped a satisfactory crop, and most of the mealies she required for household purposes she bought from the people around."

Another of her friends from this time onwards was Dr. J. Victor Hartley, the District Surgeon, who writes of her:

" As District Surgeon of Tsomo with 26,000 natives living in it, I learnt to realise the great value of her work. Those in the vicinity of her home were among the most backward and wild unsophisticated children of nature, practically untouched by civilisation, indulging in their native customs and rites—many very immoral—and beer-drinking feasts, with the resultant affrays, and steeped in superstition, affording a happy hunting-ground for heathen doctors and doctoresses, many of whom in secret still practised witchcraft—raw material of the toughest! But she had little sense of fear. Her force of character was such that the raw native in his wildest moments of unrestrained passion or fury, whether at a dance, a beer-drinking, or ill-using his family, always showed her respect.

" Quiet, steady, unassuming, she was very active, never content unless at work. No hill was too steep, no distance too far if a native called for advice or aid. When on duty in the Kei Hills I would often meet her alone wending her way on foot up and down the steep, rough footpaths on errands of mercy to some sick native man, woman, or child. On casually questioning the natives, their replies made me realise what a power for good her lonely life had been."

## XX

## TOILING AND REJOICING

THE years passed quietly away in patient and lowly service, her influence spreading and deepening, like leaven, in the life of the district.

The services on Sunday were well attended; in the noon Bible Class—that fascinating but anxious bit of work—were half a hundred girls; the prayer-meeting early on Wednesday morning was a favourite with the people, and "it is a good sign of the warmth of a church," she wrote, "when the prayer-meeting is well attended." There was always a goodly number of candidates under training or ready for admission to the membership. Sometimes the wives of a polygamist would come to the classes desiring earnestly to join the fellowship of believers. To arrange such matters was always a little difficult, and Mrs. Forsyth was often sorry for the women. One for whom she had much regard became depressed at her position and a look of sadness settled upon her face. Naturally in such a state of society odd complications cropped up in the development of the infant church. One of her ablest helpers, for instance, was a convert with three heathen sons, two of whom were married to Christian women.

There continued to be numerous conversions. Even the witch-doctors were attracted by what was more wonderful than their "magic," and not a few abandoned their evil practices and became converts. One woman who had held grimly out for nineteen years against 'Smoyana's entreaties came at last to her with a broken and contrite heart. She was never elated when such victories were won; she was only humbly grateful, giving thanks to God. Many a meeting of thanksgiving she held for all that was being done in the district. Not that she was ever satisfied with what was achieved. She wanted not "drops," but "big showers" of blessing. Her vision, too, had expanded. It used to be confined to Xolobe; then she took in Africa; now her range swept over the entire world. She exhorted her friends to the same service. "Pray," she wrote, "for Xolobe. Pray for Africa. Pray for the world."

## TOILING AND REJOICING 163

She never sought, however, to hide the dark side of the picture. Black hours she had in abundance. Women would be forced back into heathenism. There would be suspensions from the membership. Promising girls would be tempted and fall away. An epidemic of beer-drinking would undo months and even years of laborious toil. She would go into a hut and find children in the agony of some disease and the girls in attendance lying drunk.

One woman nearly broke her heart. She had a son who became a good scholar and could read the Kafir Bible. When he expressed a wish to become a Christian his mother went about the district saying scandalous things against the saint in the mission-house. Then she engaged a Kafir *igqira* to doctor her boy, with the result that he plunged into sin and became one of the wildest and most reckless youths in Xolobe. Three other children came to the school and showed a bias towards the new way. The mother withdrew them at once and burned the clothes of the eldest, making her go naked. " Is it not enough for you to go to hell," said 'Smoyana bitterly, " but you must drag down your children with you ? " Nevertheless she continued for years to go to the woman's hut, only to be received with rude and impertinent words.

One day she asked her, " What *is* taking the place of God in your heart ? "

To her surprise the answer was, " God has the chief place, Ma."

" How can I believe that," replied 'Smoyana incredulously, " when I see that charm round your neck, and those brass rings on your arms ? "

Next time she went to the hut the ornaments were gone.

" We are praying every night," the woman said, " and saying grace before meals." By and by she surrendered herself completely.

She was very downcast when, having sought to win some heathen heart, she failed. Her nearest neighbour on the height above the mission-house was a heathen. He became very ill. But he would not see her, and refused the help she wished to render him. " I want to have nothing to do with your Jesus," he said. He was attended by a witch-doctor who spoilt both mind and body. " It is one of the saddest sights I have ever seen," she declared.

Natural visitations continued frequently to impede the work.

Drought wrought havoc with the pros-

## TOILING AND REJOICING

perity of the cultivators, and Xolobe was quarantined for two years on account of the ravages of East Coast cattle fever. When rain failed prayer-meetings were organised, and they never seemed in vain. Her oldest elder—still after twenty-five years' service as true and staunch as ever—used often to take the leading part. " We are just like little birds in a nest," he would say, " sitting with open mouths waiting the coming of the mother-bird to receive."

During a dust-storm, followed by heavy rain, a woman took refuge at the mission-house. It was her old boarder Ida, who had been on a journey and had been caught in the storm some miles away. Mrs. Forsyth was pleased to see her looking so bright and cheerful. She had married a Christian young man, a Wesleyan teacher and preacher who came of fine stock, and continued to teach in his school. She was now on her way to visit his people who were very fond of her. " She is quite a credit to the ladies," wrote Mrs. Forsyth to Greenock.

The greater part of her day was taken up with visiting from kraal to kraal. Soon after breakfast she made ready. The dinner was prepared and set on to cook and then left to look after itself. Carrying a large black sunshade—on which she sometimes fixed a white cover—and a bag over her arm containing her Bible and hymn-book, she set out, either alone or accompanied by her servant. Whenever on the steep tracts she met a man, woman, or child she acted, unconsciously, the part of the Ancient Mariner and constrained them to stop and listen. Under the spell of that calm face and those bright eyes they could not choose but hear.

It was the same in the huts where the sick and the aged were her special care. After a few words of kindly enquiry she read a portion of Scripture; then came an earnest talk, followed by hymn and prayer. She would then direct her maid to prepare a cup of tea out of the small packet she had brought for the invalid. With more kind words she said farewell and went on to the next kraal.

Here she would find all the adults away at a heathen dance or beer-drinking, and only the boys and girls about. These she would gather together, teaching them a hymn or making them repeat the Lord's Prayer, and telling them about the gracious Saviour who loved little children.

And so the day would pass. In the late afternoon she would return tired and hungry

CHRISTIAN FINGO GIRLS
Ida is on the extreme left

A HEATHEN FAMILY

## TOILING AND REJOICING 167

to find the fire out and the dinner cold, and her black cat—which considered itself the most important member of the household—yawning with ennui.

"On one occasion," writes Miss Auld, "after Presbytery meetings at Paterson, before the missionaries had scattered, I rode up with two of them—my Father (Mr. Auld of Columba) and Mr. Hunter of Gillespie to see Mrs. Forsyth. We had not told her we were coming, and when we reached the house we found it closed. We heard from a man passing that Mrs. Forsyth had gone to visit some sick person about a mile away. We followed. When we rode up to the hut we saw her seated inside on a stump of wood, deep in conversation with the old sick heathen man. She looked tired and very heated after her uphill walk, but she was all smiles of welcome as soon as she saw us. She came out and we sat at the side of the hut in the shade chatting. Then she asked the missionaries to go into the hut and have a few words of prayer with the old man. As we mounted our horses she started out for home carrying her bag of books and leaning heavily upon her stout staff. She looked a lonely woman."

Many would have counted her life grey

and monotonous, but she never felt it to be so because she was doing the work, not for her own gain or profit, but for her Master, and her toil was lightened and irradiated by her love for Him. Service in this spirit is always happiness.

# XXI

## PERSONAL CHARACTERISTICS

In manner our heroine was quiet and gentle, with a gracious humility of demeanour blended with the dignity of a shy reserve. " There was no pose or pretence about her," says one who visited her; " no one would dream of believing that *she* would box any one's ears." Neither her long years of loneliness nor her contact with the vilest elements in primitive nature had made her any less a gentlewoman in thought and action.

" Mrs. Forsyth," remarked a trader's wife, " is a marvellous woman, living all alone like that; it is wonderful what some people will do for a hobby ! "

She was not, however, lonely in the higher sense. When she was asked if she never found the isolation and loneliness oppressive, she quietly replied, " I am never alone." Her Master was very real and close to her; He was her intimate companion and counsellor, and she turned to Him as naturally as to a living friend. When baffled by opposition and difficulties, " we just go and tell Jesus about our troubles," she said.

Prayer to her was no formal or stated experience; it was perpetual communion; the atmosphere in which her soul lived. She believed in petition and answer as simply as a child, and hence her intercession was of the most definite character. One of the reasons why she went into details so minutely, and mentioned so many names in her letters and reports, was that her friends in Scotland might pray for individual cases, and she had implicit faith in their supplications. Once she was solicitous about two heathen women. They came to a prayer-meeting, and there suddenly made public confession. This, she noted with delight, was on the day set apart for Africa by the Prayer Union of the Church at home. She was a member of the Union and a firm believer in its silent and potent influence. It was interesting to visitors to note that when giving thanks at meals, or at family worship—and often in conversation—she would in her absorbed moments drop from English into Kafir as if it better expressed her emotion.

Her attitude of dependence made her

## PERSONAL CHARACTERISTICS 171

grateful for the least gleam of sunshine that fell across her path. She saw God's hand in every little event, and was continually on her knees praising and rejoicing. One day she sent two girls a message. A thunderstorm, tropical in its intensity, came on, and the river rose. They could not cross. Seizing waterproof and umbrella 'Smoyana went to their aid and actually endeavoured to ford the raging water, but could only go far enough to throw them a plaid. She thought they would be washed away and turned to make another attempt when two natives appeared and got them over. " How good God is ! " she exclaimed. " What a grateful trio gathered round the family altar that night to return thanks ! "

Her interest in the doings of the world was always keen and kept her mind fresh and active. She read the papers and magazines sent to her from the first cover to the last, her special favourites being *The Record*, and *Women's Missionary Magazine* of her own Church, the *British Weekly*, the *Life of Faith*, and the *Quiver*. She followed the continued stories in the *Quiver* with great zest, for she had a romantic strain in her, and a very human and womanly liking for the tender side of life, and she was never happier than when aiding and abetting some love affair. She saw romance even in a native wedding which to others appeared only the settlement of a painfully prosaic bargain, a mere matter of buying and selling. She would give up the entire mission-house to the parties and treat them as honoured guests. And if the ring had been forgotten, or if it dropped and rolled away, or if the gifts were not of the kind usually presented at a marriage she kept her countenance—though not without difficulty.

For she had that indispensable quality in a missionary, a saving sense of humour. She saw the light side even of her troubles and would smile them away. Often her eyes would dance and her whole body shake with laughter so that others would be infected by her spirit and join in the merriment. She enjoyed fun even when it was at her own expense, and her very simplicity of nature laid her open to pleasantry. Once when she was unwell, Miss Auld, with thoughtful kindness, sent her up some scones, bottled fruit, and a bottle of home-made lemon syrup. Next day a note came down thanking her for the gift and especially for the medicine. " I am taking it," she said, " and I am finding it is doing me good."

## PERSONAL CHARACTERISTICS 173

The next time Miss Auld saw her she asked, "What medicine was that you referred to in your note?" Thereupon she produced the bottle which had contained the lemon syrup saying, "There were no directions on it so I took a spoonful after each meal!" "You took it as it was—neat?" exclaimed Miss Auld in an awed voice. "Just as it was; and I felt the better of it." Miss Auld declared that it was a clear case of faith-healing!

Her charity was equal to her simplicity. She was the living embodiment of the thirteenth chapter of first Corinthians. Kindness she found to be the best key to unlock the hearts of an affectionate people, and ridicule a more powerful weapon than abuse. In her judgement of the native character she was just without being severe, and was ready with excuses for delinquents, never being better pleased than when she could relate some incident to their credit. She used to tell of an old man whom she knew. In his household were a son and grandson. Then came a daughter and daughter-in-law and five children. Three friends from Cape Colony arrived on a long visit. Next a brother died, and the hut in which he had stored all the food was burned down. The old man at once brought his sister-in-law and her five children to his home. This made eighteen persons to cater and work for, but the old gentleman bore his burden bravely and never grumbled. " And he was a heathen," said Mrs. Forsyth.

Overflowing with a kindness unrestricted by thought of self, spending nothing on her own comfort, her life was a perpetual effort to serve others. Her bounty knew no limit, and her hospitality was often startling in its prodigality. If you were a visitor you would be welcomed from afar, and her kind hands would be held out to draw you into the shelter of the house. You would find the table groaning with provisions, and you were no friend of hers if you did not do justice to the fare. Strangers were usually warned at Paterson to partake liberally when they arrived. On one occasion after soup and a course of fowls and vegetables a baked custard was brought to the table in a huge enamelled bedroom basin, and proved to be as delicious in quality as it was prodigious in size. She never failed to have a cup of tea ready for visitors when they arrived after the hot journey over the hills. At the annual meeting of the Women's Christian Association, of which she became President,

## PERSONAL CHARACTERISTICS 175

she would kill a sheep or pig and entertain the members to a generous feast.

When alone, however, she lived sparingly. She was a good housekeeper, economical in her methods, and baked her own bread. "That is one thing I can boast of," she would say with a smile. "I am a fine baker."

She rose at six and at seven had breakfast, which consisted usually of bread and butter and eggs. Dinner was nominally at one, but as this was the best time of the day for visiting the kraals she was seldom in to eat it; the courses were soup and mealies and milk, with sometimes pudding in addition. At five she had tea with bread and scones. She partook of no supper and retired at eight, but often later.

About dress she cared little and was a law unto herself so far as fashion was concerned, her first consideration being her own comfort. There were no shops to tempt her and no critics to please, and her attire was as plain as she could well make it. Her boots, several sizes too large for her, were an eyesore to Miss Auld, who pleaded in vain for the adoption of a neater pair.

Her homely motherliness made her the idol of the people. Every one, "dressed" or "red," was welcome at the school-house.

She was never too busy to see and talk to those who called. Women came at all hours to pour out their troubles to her, or to ask for assistance. One Sunday morning at five o'clock there was a knock at the door. She sprang out of bed and answered it. It was a heathen woman with a little child. " 'Smoyana," she said, " I want a dress for my little one. I want her to go to church." She received it. Passers-by would come and ask for water to quench their thirst, or an ash to light a pipe, and would have their request granted and go away with a word or two of kindly counsel. Children brought their slates and books and left them with her to be called for next morning on their way to school, and they never went away without a slice of bread or a handful of cooked mealies.

She was naturally so open-handed, so generous, and so confiding that she never learnt to suspect others or to safeguard her own interests, and was consequently often taken advantage of, but this she did not mind. Even in little things her faith received many a mild shock. Once she reported a " leakage " of cups and saucers, knives and forks. " Perhaps," she said, " I have been to blame myself as I ' trusted ' and did not lock up anything."

# XXII

## A VISION OF SOULS

ONE night, twenty-five years after she had begun her task in Xolobe, Mrs. Forsyth sat alone in her little dwelling on the hill-top, her Bible on her lap, her mind meditating quietly on her work. Methodical in habit she knew the exact extent of it—the number of those in the fellowship of the church, the membership of the various classes, the size of the day school. She knew also how many of the heathen still remained to be won. But what could statistics tell of the real successes and failures?

Her thoughts began to turn back and wander over the years. Memories came crowding upon her. She saw, in long array, men, women, and children whom she had prayed for, and influenced and saved. She also saw others who had gone their own way despite all her endeavour. It was a gallery of souls, and as she paused before each she smiled or grew sad as she recalled their histories. Vivid little portraits they were, vignettes, so to speak, of heathen life and conditions, giving the real colour and feeling, the humour and the pathos, which figures could never supply.

Here are some of the pictures she saw in vision that night as the mists were gathering in the valley and as the shadows were settling down upon her own life.

### The Reformation of Qualini

The senior elder was at one time a wandering ne'er-do-weel about Xolobe, always drunk, and given over to heathen practices. He was found sleeping on the edge of a precipice overlooking the church. Influenced by Mrs. Forsyth he gradually reformed and was baptized and took the name of John, becoming known thereafter as John Mbanga. He brought in his wife and all his family into the church. An earnest and impressive preacher, he became Mrs. Forsyth's principal helper in the work for thirty years.

### A Fine Record

Gungubele was one of the better type of heathen lads; he was a boy of twelve when

## A VISION OF SOULS 179

Mrs. Forsyth first met him at his father's kraal. When he grew up he married a heathen wife and they had a beautiful child, a girl, who entwined herself round their hearts. Her death was a severe blow, and in his grief the father turned to that God whom he had hitherto despised, and found comfort. A touch of ambition sent him to learn to read. His books were beside him morning, noon, and night; he even went to the school, and sat amongst the children, whom, owing to his determination and diligence, he soon outstripped. His Bible became his constant companion. When he was received into the fellowship of the church he chose the name of Joseph. He exercised an immense influence over the heathen, and his wife soon became one in mind with him. Not content with being a silent witness to the truth, he became a worker in the church, and succeeded in bringing no fewer than twenty-seven of his relatives to Christ, including his father's two widows and his three sisters. Drawn to Johannesburg by prospects of better work, he returned at Mrs. Forsyth's request and was elected an elder and preached alternately with Mbanga.

## A Model Family

Another elder was Siyo Jonas who came to Xolobe a widower, and a bold wild heathen. He was converted while at work, and cast in his lot with the Christians and joined the church. Marrying a Christian girl, who made him an excellent wife, he studied hard, and was soon able to read the Bible fluently and preach with great power. He was ultimately made the evangelist for the district. His daughters attended the Sunday School and took many prizes, and one went to Lovedale to study to be a teacher. One day three came quietly to the candidates' class and gave themselves to Christ. Jonas was a great help to Mrs. Forsyth. His example might have influenced his two brothers at the same kraal, but they preferred their old ways.

## From Lion to Lamb

One of the most reckless and uproarious characters of Xolobe was Myanga; none so rough and noisy as he on his way to the heathen orgies of a Saturday evening. Suddenly the spell of the gospel fell upon him; the lion was transformed into the lamb;

# A VISION OF SOULS 181

none now so meek and gentle as he. He became an earnest witness to the truth, preaching by word and example, and was greatly helped by his wife, a fine girl from the Sunday class, who brought up her young family as carefully as the strictest Scottish mother could have done.

### A Notable Transformation

Another notable case was that of Mazawazi, a woman of great force of character and energy, but considered the most hardened sinner in the district. " Never was any other woman so haughty and contemptuous of all who approached her with the gospel," says Mrs. Forsyth. She was converted and became a changed woman, and her heathen neighbours gazed at her and marvelled.

### Back to Red Clay

Lolo was 'Smoyana's near neighbour, a heathen, proud and obstinate, who hated the new way of life and would have nothing to do with it. He refused even to speak with her about it; whenever she began he either kept silent or put her off in one way or another or walked away. Let her talk about any other subject and he was voluble and agreeable, but let her trend on his customs and superstitions and his mouth snapped obstinately and he remained dour and unapproachable.

His wife was even worse, and with her the patient missionary had often a bad time.

Once their little girl was ill and at the point of death. Impatiently the wife cried to her eldest daughter, "Take that child out of my sight. I cannot bear her cough-coughing." The girl lifted the child up, swung her on her back, and tramped to the hut of an aunt who was a Christian. The aunt, and a daughter-in-law who was there at the time, looked in pity on the wasted form of the sick child, and the latter knelt down and prayed earnestly that she might be spared. From that moment the girl began to recover, and in a few months was able to return to her home. Clad in a pink print dress which her friends had given her, she was an attractive girl, but when she arrived at the hut her mother looked askance at her, demanded why she was wearing the Christian dress, and ultimately persuaded her to throw it aside and resume the red clay.

Her sister was of a different temperament. The Bible lessons from the teacher, Jonathan

## A VISION OF SOULS

Koyanas, in school had made her a Christian, and despite the strenuous efforts of the family she kept to her resolution and walked her own way. She became engaged and went to a Christian home, but her parents and the rest of the family remained in their semi-savage state.

### The Discarded Wife

Matshoba was a typical heathen with two wives and a large family. One of the wives appeared at the station. " I want clothes," she said; " I want to be a Christian." That she was in earnest was proved by her changed life. Her example so impressed her husband that he also discarded his heathen beliefs, and by and by the whole family became disciples. When Matshoba, according to the law of the church, had to make the choice between his wives he married the second, who was young and pretty. But the elder woman showed the reality of her faith by continuing to minister to the family, and the eldest son was particularly kind and gentle towards her in her enforced widowhood.

### The Dumb Boy who spoke

Matshoba had a nephew called Maliwe, a wild boy, deaf and dumb, who was not wanted by his friends. Mrs. Forsyth employed him to bring milk to the station and found him clever, willing, and trustworthy. As he sometimes came when she was out she was in the habit of leaving the door open in order that he might deposit it inside. Once the can did not look clean, and when Maliwe appeared for it she took up some earth and flung it into the vessel to signify that it was dirty. He began to labour under the stress of some strong emotion, and to her surprise exclaimed, " *y-Inkwenkwe* "—" it was the boy." It was the first time he had spoken, and he never afterwards uttered another word.

So attached did he become to 'Smoyana that he indicated his wish to leave his heathen friends and embrace Christianity. The Paterson *umfundisi* and teacher both questioned him by signs and were satisfied as to his sincerity and put him on probation. The outward and visible indication of his inward change was the donning of a white nightgown and a big waterproof cloak, but later, when Mr. Davidson admitted him to church fellowship, he was more respectably

# A VISION OF SOULS

attired. He proved a faithful disciple. By watching the teacher pronouncing the letters he had some notion of the alphabet, and at worship he prayed in his own fashion, endeavouring to speak, but making strange sounds. " But," as Mrs. Forsyth observed, " it is not with the lips but with the heart that prayer is made to God."

Maliwe, like many another native, was drawn into the life and work of the mines, and did not long survive the experience.

### Self-exiled

When a native became a Christian he was subjected to a good deal of ridicule and persecution at the hands of his unregenerate neighbours and friends, and, not unnaturally, he sought to find a new sphere where he could live at peace. This was the case with Lalapi, a fine character who heard the gospel from Mrs. Forsyth, and accepted it, and whose wife soon followed his example. His land was not very productive and, this providing an excuse, he removed to Cape Colony, where he got on well. Mrs. Forsyth, however, thought that Christian natives should remain where they were and try to influence their neighbours.

## Out of the Furnace

One day Mrs. Forsyth was tramping over the hills when she saw a strange-looking creature sitting in the grass. It was a youth called Jongelanga. His face was painted white, and he wore a whitened sheepskin; he had been taking part in the initiation ceremony which ruins so many for life. Some time later she saw him at the services and prayer-meeting, and it was not long before he repented and decided to throw in his lot with the Christians. Big as he was he attended school and learnt to read and delighted to pore over the Bible. Anxious to marry a fine-looking girl, he went away to work to earn a dowry and on his return they were wedded. She died leaving him with two children and he married again, another school-girl, a member of the church. He became a deacon and joint treasurer and preached with great simplicity and earnestness. One of his self-imposed tasks was to improve and beautify the church-grounds.

## Miriam's Stand

Lolo Pama, a heathen, took his daughter Miriam from school in order that she might

## A VISION OF SOULS 187

take part, along with an older sister, in the degrading ceremony which initiates girls into womanhood. Protests and prayers seemed of no avail. " If she does not go into the custom," said her father, " she will die." Her clothes had worn out and he refused to buy more. Just then a box arrived from a Girls' Auxiliary at home and she received what she required to maintain her self-respect. A few weeks later Mrs. Forsyth was delighted to be told that all the efforts of her parents and friends had failed to make Miriam " red "; she was so good and brave and industrious that they had left her alone, and her father had even bought her Christian clothes. Then her young sister was taken seriously ill with inflammation of the lungs. " I do not want to see her die," said the mother; " take her to her aunt." Miriam carried her to this woman, who was a Christian, and prayer was offered on the child's behalf. She recovered. When her mother saw her again she exclaimed, " Take off her red clothes and put them in the fire. Here is a shilling to buy a dress." More money was added, and the girl appeared in church wearing a pretty pink print.

### The Leg of Mutton

One day looking down the valley Mrs. Forsyth saw a little child weighed down with some kind of burden toiling up the steep ascent. When she arrived the load turned out to be a leg of mutton which she had brought as a gift to 'Smoyana. Deliwe, as the girl was called, was a heathen from a heathen town, with a mother who was kind enough but liable to violent fits of temper. She continued at the school until she was twelve. Though of an affectionate and docile nature she did not change her ways, and when she married it was to a " red." Only when her eyes began to trouble her and she was threatened with loss of sight did she remember the teaching she had received and became a Christian. From that time her eyesight improved. A younger sister in the school became a Christian and took her place in the choir. After baptism she received the name of Elizabeth and married well.

### Sister and Brother

Elizabeth had an inseparable companion called Mildred, the only daughter of a witch-doctor, a lovable girl whose apparently mild

## A VISION OF SOULS 189

disposition belied her strength of character. She made great progress in school and was, like Elizabeth, a fine sewer and baker. When she resolved to join the Christians' lot her parents, who were very fond of her, could not find it in their heart to oppose her wish. Her situation, however, was not a happy one, and Mrs. Forsyth was often sorry for her. At the beer-drinkings she would sit apart, lonely and shunned, until the festivities were over. She was received into the church at the same time as Elizabeth.

Mildred's brother also passed through the school and obtained the prize for Bible knowledge. Troubled like many about his deeper life he consulted Mrs. Forsyth. " I have two people within me," he said. " One urges me to do bad things, and the other urges me to do good things." 'Smoyana explained how it was and begged him to heed the prompting of the Divine spirit. Knowing something of what was passing in his mind his heathen mother called in a witch-doctor who used all his craft and strangled his good inclinations. After he left school he became a wild and reckless youth.

### Suiting the Action to the Word

Mlonyeni came with his aged grandmother to reside in Xolobe. He was one of the rawest and most ignorant of men. Soon he came under the influence of the white woman. " Teach me to pray," he said to her. She looked at him and the words of the beautiful Psalm came to her mind : "*Hide Thy face from my sins and blot out all mine iniquities. Create in me a clean heart and renew a right spirit within me.*" She began to repeat it as the best prayer he could utter.

" *Hide thy face.*"

" Yes, mum," he said, covering up his features—he thought this was a preliminary requirement.

He was baptized along with his grandmother and made a good recruit, sometimes accompanying 'Smoyana on her rounds of the huts and praying fervently.

### The Live Coal

" Can I not take just a little beer ? " asked a heathen woman who attended the services in her " red " clothes. " Well," was the reply, " if you take a very little live coal into your bosom will it not burn you ? " She saw the force of the argument and

# A VISION OF SOULS 191

resolved to give up beer altogether. A beautiful woman with a gentle nature she became a regular attender at church and was the soul of lovingkindness to every one. Her sister, on the other hand, was bold and bad. At every beer-drinking she was the worst and the most violent of the company. She, too, was influenced by 'Smoyana in so marked a degree that her very face changed, and she became notable for her meek and attractive expression.

### A Scene at Sunrise

The scene is a Kafir hut on a summer morning at sunrise. The floor is well swept, the hearth is tidy, there is a neat rack for knobkerries, a coil of newly-made grass rope hangs on the wall, and everything bears the unusual mark of a cleanly and industrious home-maker. Sitting on some tastefully-made rush mats are the White Mother and a company of Christian women quietly engaged in praying for the gentle and refined housewife who lies on her death-bed. After some comforting words are spoken the low feeble tones of the woman are heard, " Oh God, I plead for mercy. Do not despise me although I am a poor heathen. I cast myself on Thee."

The gathering breaks up but she continues in prayer and passes away murmuring, " I am going home."

### Rorela

Rorela was the daughter of a hardened heathen. A friendly school-girl brought her to the mission-house and asked for a frock that she might be able to come to school. Her happiness in her new possession was short-lived, for her mother tore it off when she returned and despatched it back to the school-house. She grew up a heathen and married a heathen. Mrs. Forsyth pleaded with her to send her girl, a bright child, to school. Rorela went off in a rage. Not long after she gave in and became a disciple.

### A Brave Girl

This is in Mrs. Forsyth's own words: " One of our girls, Martha, was enticed by her guardian to go with him to Tsitsa. He hired a wagon to take her and her sister there against my wishes. I objected for two reasons: first because she was leaving her aged grandmother who had brought her up, and whom her guardian did not recom-

# A VISION OF SOULS 193

pense as he ought to have done; second, because she was not going to a Christian home. When Martha got there she found a red man, ready with a large dowry of cattle expecting her hand in marriage. The first condition was that she must renounce her Christianity and put on red clay. This Martha refused to do. They tried to compel her; but although they stole her clothes, she told them she would go home just as she was. A respectable young man from Xolobe helped her. She had to return on foot and cross several rivers on the way. The journey took ten days. Weary and footsore she arrived safely at home, guided through each perplexing path, and sheltered beneath the covering wings."

### ASKED OF GOD

Noventi Nkuhlu was in great sorrow. All her children, with a few exceptions, had died at their birth. One, born after she was converted, was spared and she named him Pendulu, or "Answered." She asked her heathen husband to have a thanksgiving service at the kraal and he consented. The day was cold and stormy, but the large hut was filled with women, both Christian and "red." Many fervent prayers were offered, and there was a general opinion that the child should be dedicated to God. When the father came to the mission-house to register the birth he asked cautiously if the baptism cost anything. "No," was the reply. "Then," he said, "I give the child to you." "Not to me," replied Mrs. Forsyth; "to God." "All right—give him his name." The one appropriately chosen was Samuel.

### LALAPI

When Mr. Buchanan visited Xolobe, amongst the school children who sang a sweet Kafir hymn was a heathen boy named Lalapi. He was later taken away but Mrs. Forsyth saw him occasionally. Marrying a heathen girl he made his home in a solitary spot in the mountains. One day Mrs. Forsyth saw a stranger in church and afterwards found it to be Lalapi. He had been converted and wished to learn to read in order that he might be able to con the Bible for himself.

# A VISION OF SOULS

### Hard Hearts

Kas Nkuhlu was a heathen who always rose and walked away when 'Smoyana approached his place, and never listened to Christian preaching if he could help it. He hugged his heathen pleasures and would not give them up, and she could make nothing of him. And yet he had a Christian woman for his chief wife.

For seven years 'Smoyana visited an aged heathen once a week, but his heart was like flint. When he was about ninety years of age he attended a beer-drinking where his excesses made him so ill that he was taken home in a cart. He lived on many years and died as he had lived. One of his sons was a witch-doctor and was stabbed to death; another, also a witch-doctor, died suddenly when absent from the district; a third, who followed the same calling, lost his foot in an accident and died soon after.

# PART III
## EVENTIDE

AGE 67-74

# I

## COMPLETELY SHUT IN

WHEN Mrs. Forsyth ceased her visits to Paterson the only link she had with the outer world was snapped. She had been in the habit of going there every quarter for Communion, but latterly she began to feel that her strength was not sufficient for the long and rough pilgrimage. One of her last journeys indicated that the time had come when she must relinquish what had always been a pleasant break in her life and a stimulating spiritual experience.

She set out from Xolobe on Saturday afternoon. A strong wind was blowing and dark clouds were looming up in the sky. She had not proceeded far when a severe thunderstorm burst over the land, the rain lashing down in torrents and forcing her to take shelter in the nearest kraal. When she started again the long wet grass and the muddy paths completed her discomfiture, but she trudged steadily on until she arrived at the hut of a Christian woman with whom she had arranged to stay the night. Here she disposed of her soaked garments and was made comfortable.

A little old native woman slipped in and lay on the floor. She was an invalid with a weak back who had also come to the hut to remain overnight on her way to Communion. " It is my first," she said, " but I am afraid the elders won't accept me. I haven't been able to attend the candidates' class very regularly." 'Smoyana assured her that they would not take this into account, but in any case she would explain matters to them.

Her first thoughts on the lovely Sunday morning were ones of hope and thanksgiving. The invalid and she set out early, walking slowly in and out of the mealie fields, the Kafir corn being sometimes a foot above their heads. Very pleased was the old native woman that her companion often paused to admire things and to rest, but she did not know that 'Smoyana, watching her with her deep kind eyes, noticed how trying the walking was for her, and purposely made occasion to linger for her sake.

The sweet tones of the church bell were ringing out over hill and valley as they

## COMPLETELY SHUT IN 201

approached Paterson, and when they entered the building they found fourteen elders on the platform and a bright and happy congregation. Her thoughts went back to the year 1879 when she first saw the people, and she contrasted their clean and well-clad appearance now with their ragged clothes and uncouth demeanour then. Her old friend was received into fellowship with nineteen others. After the service many of the members came to greet her, and then she returned as leisurely as she had come, pondering over the solemn service, and recalling the words of a great Scottish preacher: " We are permitted to ascend to the gate of heaven that we may descend to the depths with the blessings received in order that we may bless others."

Isolated before, she was now completely shut in. Apart from the Aulds she rarely had a white visitor. Only once, in 1912, do we get a glimpse of her. This was when a hurried call was made by the Rev. Robert Mure, the missionary at Ross, Umtata, who writes :

" I started on horseback one bright hot summer's day from Paterson in company with the Rev. William Auld. There seemed no direct cart-track, only a sheep-track.

After an hour's riding the path became too precipitous and difficult for horseback, and we dismounted and led our horses on foot for a quarter of an hour. Another hour's riding brought us to Xolobe out-station. It is nothing to boast of, nothing to look at. The country round about is mountainous with patches of bush here and there. While not very picturesque it has a certain grandeur and variety of scenery. Xolobe itself consists of a tin school-house, a few Kafir huts, and Mrs. Forsyth's small two-roomed house, little better than many Kafir houses, though quite clean and tidy and comfortable enough in a plain way—no amenities, no trees, no gardens, nothing but the veld and the Kafirs and the burnt grass and the glaring sun.

"We dismounted at the door and she was there to welcome us. The homely frankness, the honest truth-speaking face, the open, clear, direct discourse, all with a strong Scottish flavour, was most impressive and striking, especially in that spot full of subtle and too often false-tongued Kafirs.

"How direct the questions, how simple and to the point! The exact place from which I had come; my field of labour; my health; was I married; how many children? Then a few simple expressions of thanks for

## COMPLETELY SHUT IN 203

the privilege of a visit in this remote place from a minister, nay, two ministers. There was no talk of shop, no comparing of notes about conversions among the heathen.

" A cup of tea was served to us. Then I conducted family worship. A handshake, and we were off into the veld again and she was left alone—a white woman among the blacks."

## II

## HER INDEPENDENCE

THERE were kind hearts in Scotland always solicitous for the welfare of the lonely missionary. The Greenock ladies never ceased to think of her and plan for her. Without the advantage of personal touch with the people in whom they took an interest, with nothing but quarterly statements of bare facts to stimulate them, they yet gave regularly to her work, not grudgingly but liberally and with enthusiasm.

Others also thought of her and sent her help—many who knew nothing about her save that she was a lonely pioneer of the gospel bravely struggling amidst a heathen people. Gifts came from a band of young working women. Twelve shillings came from two poor girls " with real prayerful interest and love." A box of napery, blankets, and wearing apparel for her personal use arrived

## HER INDEPENDENCE 205

from the members of her old congregation at Cairneyhill.

This wealth of effort, this outpouring of sympathy, so unselfish, so loyal, was in its way almost as wonderful as her own service. The Greenock ladies were but types of that great multitude of honourable women throughout Scotland who are continuously busy with the self-imposed task of ministering to the needs of missionaries abroad. Little is publicly made known about their gracious activities; the work is accomplished quietly, almost privately, within the sphere of work-parties, Sabbath Schools, and girls' classes, and by families and circles of friends. It is all done in the spirit of Christ, gladly and lovingly, and for His sake who did so much for Women.

However generous the intentions of the ladies were they were often at a loss how to minister to her comfort. Whenever South African missionaries came home on furlough the first question put to them was: " What can we do for Mrs. Forsyth—is she needing anything?" They were well aware she would not accept money for her own use. On one occasion they sent her a generous gift and afterwards saw the amount acknowledged in the *Record* of the Church as a contribution from her towards a special missionary effort. " She is the most unselfish and independent person imaginable," said Miss Macfarlane.

But now and again they endeavoured, almost surreptitiously, to send out little articles that might conduce to her well-being. When Mrs. Stewart was home she suggested a table-lamp, and this she herself conveyed out, though with more and more misgiving as she approached Kafraria. They also consulted Miss Auld when she was in Scotland, and on her recommendation resolved to despatch a bath and an easy-chair to Xolobe. On Miss Auld's return to Paterson she dropped a casual hint as to what was coming, whereupon Mrs. Forsyth reached hastily for pen and paper and wrote to Miss Macfarlane :

" We have excellent bathing facilities here, and an easy-chair would be a cumbersome thing to get here, as there is no traffic by wagon, so if you would not be offended I would rather not receive them. We have an excellent water-supply within five minutes' walk of the house."

Later, however, when she grew feebler, and was unable to go to the river, she proposed to buy a bath. Miss Auld hurried one up from Paterson for her use until she could

SMOYANA'S BATHING-PLACE

## HER INDEPENDENCE 207

procure another, on behalf of the Greenock ladies, from the nearest store, and congratulated herself on at last having achieved a distinct victory over the scruples of her friend. And when she was actually permitted to sit beside 'Smoyana and darn her stockings she felt that the citadel of independence, hitherto so impregnable, had fallen at last!

Every penny received was accounted for. With the proceeds from the boxes of goods sent out — she sold the clothing to the natives — donations were given to needy causes in the neighbouring fields. When she left there was a balance of £25 to her credit in this connection, and she handed it over for repairs to Xolobe church. Once when she had a sum of 10s. in hand she was at a loss what to do with it, and then wrote to Miss Macfarlane: " I will get boots for Su-pi, a poor girl who is usually first at the early prayer-meeting, even on stormy mornings. All the girls have boots, Su-pi has none, and her feet are swollen with cold." Su-pi, it will be recalled, was the granddaughter of Taki.

She was latterly much troubled by the thought that she had accepted money from the Greenock ladies in support of her native servant. The understanding in her mind was that the servant was also to be a Bible-woman, and her scrupulous conscience now made it appear as if the disciple had obtained greater service than her Master. In distress she informed Miss Auld that she must pay back £51 to the ladies.

"You must not do anything of the kind," exclaimed Miss Auld. "The first desire of the ladies is that you should have efficient help and be well served in your declining years. I know that this is their wish, and they will be very vexed if you offer to send them back any of their money."

"But I am sure that the pains and rheumatism I suffer from are God's hand upon me for having taken this money under a mistake," Mrs. Forsyth persisted.

"No! no! So far from being God's hand of chastisement upon you, they are the natural outcome of a life spent strenuously in His service. At your age, and lacking all care and comfort, you cannot expect perfect health."

By degrees Miss Auld's practical wisdom prevailed, and assurance and peace came back to the gentle old missionary.

## III

## THE SHOCK OF THE WAR

IN view of her advanced age and the hard and strenuous life she had lived, her relatives in Scotland thought she might now very well relinquish her work and settle with them at home. The approach of the centenary of Dr. Livingstone, in which she took much interest, seemed an appropriate opportunity for persuading her to make up her mind on the point, and one of her nephews without her knowledge applied to the Foreign Mission Committee of the Church for a passage for her that she might return and be present at the celebrations. When she heard of this arrangement she cancelled it.

"I am just like Miss Slessor," she wrote to Miss Macfarlane; "I cannot tear myself away. Often in my dreams I am at home, and I invariably say, 'Why did I leave Africa—how can I get back?'"

Rheumatism crippled her, and she suffered

from painful outbreaks on the feet and ankles, but she would not give in. The only concession she made was to stop her walks to the more distant kraals. She continued all her other activities, though she was noticeably much quieter and more meditative. Her Bible was her constant companion, and, as ever, her source of inspiration and strength.

Into the orderly calm of her days in 1914 came disquieting rumours of trouble in Europe, like the first tremors which denote a distant earthquake. The shock of the early news of the war told heavily upon her. She visualised the sufferings of the young men in the trenches, the greater agonies of the battle-field, their supreme sacrifice—and wept. She thought of their splendid heroism and of the self-sacrifice and unity of the people—and rejoiced. And her faith never wavered. " The Lord God Omnipotent reigneth," she said, " and He is able to restrain the wrath of man. However dark the outlook may be He can bring light out of the darkness and order out of confusion."

Comforting stricken ones at home she wrote : " I have heard it said that when a storm beats fiercely at sea and the billows rage, there are depths undisturbed beneath.

## THE SHOCK OF THE WAR 211

May it be so with your souls in this time of trouble."

As she read of the long lists of "killed in action," she said, "it was almost like the time in Egypt when there was not a house where there was not one dead."

At first the work was not affected. The Inspector of Schools failed to appear—but he was a German. The natives were quiet and unperturbed. As time went on, however, they grew a little restive and troublesome, and food-stuffs went up in price. She had to eke out her flour with mealie meal made from maize. " But," she said, " however long the war lasts, and however trying it may prove, the Lord will provide."

Despite her strong will-power the strain affected her waning vitality. In October she reached her seventieth birthday, and came to the realisation that the end had come. " I have passed the allotted span," she told her friends, " and I do not think it fair to occupy a place without being able for the duties." She mentioned to Mr. Auld that she would like to retire, but he informed her that the Foreign Mission Committee of the Church wished all missionaries to remain at their posts until the war was over. " So," she said, " I will wait until God opens the way."

The tragedy of the tremendous struggle entered her own life, her nephew, Lieutenant Moir, 1st Black Watch, being killed at Loos. " He was almost the only man I have seen," wrote out his sister, " who was really keen to go back to the front. His one fear when he was home was lest his platoon should get into action without him. He knew perfectly well, too, what he was facing. He did not consider he had the faintest chance of coming through alive in a regiment which was always in the hottest of the fighting, but he would not for a moment have wished himself elsewhere."

The blow stunned and wearied her, but she fell back on the unseen source of strength which had never failed her yet. " She is a wonderful woman," said Mr. Auld, " and keeps bright and happy under all circumstances. She is a saint."

Another fragment of news affected her sadly. " So," she writes, " poor Miss Slessor has been called home. What a loss to our mission ! I hope God will raise up some one to fill her place. I do not think there was another missionary in the world to equal her. Her heart was full of lovingkindness and tender mercy." When the story of Miss Slessor's life by the present writer was

## THE SHOCK OF THE WAR 213

published, Mrs. M'Laren sent her out a copy and she read it with delight. " I sat up all night until I finished it," she said. " I hope it will be an incentive to me to labour more abundantly and to endure hardness "—and she was seventy years of age!

## IV

## SADNESS OF FAREWELL

When, in 1915, Miss Auld returned from a visit to Scotland, she was grieved to notice the change in her old friend. She had aged perceptibly and was much thinner. Both she and her brother urged her to come and make a home with them at Paterson, where they would surround her with every comfort and bestow upon her the care and attention she needed. She would not hear of it. She preferred, she said, to end her life at Xolobe, in the belief that by her death amongst the people she would do more good than she had done in her life.

" She has led a primitive life among the heathen so long," reported Mr. Auld to the Greenock ladies, " that she dreads going back to civilised life. She has never had furlough, and is naturally reticent and shy and retiring, and there would have to be much sympathy of the silent kind shown for

## SADNESS OF FAREWELL 215

her, and due allowance made for her ways. She spends far too little on herself and too much on others. But that is just her all through; her modesty, self-effacement, and Christlikeness make us feel less than nothing compared with her. She would require to be cared for instead of caring for others as she has done all her life. We would do anything for her, and count it an honour, but it is difficult to care for her under present conditions." All that Mr. Auld could do in the circumstances was to go to Xolobe more frequently. His visits increased to one every fortnight and latterly to one every week.

It was not to be expected that Nature would suspend its inexorable process. Though her moral energy was unimpaired her physical strength weakened. "I am breaking up," she wrote in 1916. An attack of influenza left her prostrate for a month and she recovered but slowly. She lost the use of her voice. "I must give up," she decided at last; "but it will be a great wrench for me to leave my midday Sabbath class—forty-nine dear girls were present last Sabbath."

She could not trust herself to live at Paterson so near the scene of her life-labours. " If," she said, " I cannot end my days here,

I must go right away to Scotland." Her relatives, thankful to hear of her decision, at once arranged for her niece, Miss Mann, a nurse, to proceed to South Africa and bring her home. It was characteristic of her humility of mind that she wished to travel third-class in the steamer, but, needless to say, her friends would not hear of such abnegation, and the Foreign Mission Committee of the Church saw to the payment of her expenses.

It was pitiful to see her during the final days. Miss Auld says it was like watching a great tree being torn up by the roots. Several times she murmured with a quivering face, " It's not the place, it's the people I can't bear to part with." To them the parting was equally sore. " 'Smoyana," said a deputation of women who came to see her, " you are not white, you are black. Your heart is black, you are just one of ourselves." It was the highest compliment they could pay; it meant that she understood their real nature, and so was able to sympathise with and help them in their peculiar needs.

Messages of farewell began to arrive. From her old friend Mrs. Davidson came an affectionate letter : " You have," she said, " always been a very dear and good friend,

## SADNESS OF FAREWELL 217

and have been a strength and help in trouble and sorrow. I can never forget your kindness to me and mine." The native pastor, the Rev. Candlish Koti, wrote : " 'Smoyana and Xolobe are the two names that will be always associated together for many generations to come." A brief note addressed " Dear Mammy," and signed " Your loving child, Ida," intimated that her former pupil was hastening to Xolobe to say good-bye. There was no time for the missionaries of the Presbytery to do much, but they hurriedly collected a sum of money and asked her to accept it and purchase some article which would remind her of their affection and esteem.

Later, the Kafrarian Mission Council placed on record its high appreciation of her work. " Her faithful service, her complete self-surrender, her utter self-effacement, and her devotion to her Master, have been the wonder and admiration of her fellow-missionaries and many others. She will live long in the hearts of her people." And from Scotland, from the ladies on the Clyde, came, through Miss Macfarlane, the kindest of communications : " You are," they said, " worthy of the D.S.O. of the highest rank in Heaven."

## CHRISTINA FORSYTH

Her last day at Xolobe was a trying one. A farewell meeting was held to which came every soul in the district, Christian and heathen, as well as many from other outstations. Mr. Auld explained how, owing to advanced age and failing health, 'Smoyana was compelled to go back to her own land and live amongst her own people. "Never let her life and work fade amongst you, let it ever be a beacon-light showing you the road to Christ." Several natives responded saying they would never be able to forget the love of their White Mother who had come amongst them as a girl and had grown old in the service of her Master.

Then for the last time she addressed them, indulging in no personal reminiscences or self-gratulation, making no reference whatever to herself, but reiterating with passionate fervour the message which it had been her duty and happiness to proclaim all these years, and inviting them to come to the Saviour, the only source of strength and peace in this life, and the only hope for the better life to come.

With her usual hospitality she had provided a sheep and two pots of mealies as a parting feast. The crowd squatted on the grass in front of the church, and whilst they

## SADNESS OF FAREWELL 219

ate she walked in and out amongst them, shaking hands with each and saying kindly words of farewell.

Suddenly a storm gathered, the clouds broke in sheets of rain, and gathering up the fragments the people rushed into the church for shelter. Within an hour both streams were " down " and impassable. " I have never seen them rise so quickly or so fiercely," remarked Mrs. Forsyth.

When the flood-waters abated the Aulds returned to Paterson, and a lonely woman spent the evening at Xolobe in prayer.

## V

## BACK TO CIVILISATION

In the clear light of the early morning Mr. Auld again rode over the hills to Xolobe to see Mrs. Forsyth comfortably installed in the wagon. She was conveyed to Paterson by a circuitous and less rough way, Bekiwe, her old scholar and helper, accompanying her, and arrived in the evening tired and shaken in body and mind.

Having lived the life of a recluse for thirty years it was not surprising that she shrank from re-entering the world. "You don't know," she said to Miss Auld, "what an ordeal it has been for me to brace myself up even to come to Paterson."

At first she was depressed and thought she would die ere she could reach Scotland, but the unobtrusive ministrations of her host and hostess soon made her feel at ease, and after a few days the shadow lifted and her spirits revived.

The process of social acclimatisation was helped by a babe. The Rev. D. W. Semple, M.A., then of Emgwali, and his wife and child, were staying at the manse. Mrs. Forsyth was much taken with the infant who seemed always eager to come to her. This simple circumstance broke down the natural feeling of restraint which she experienced, and paved the way for pleasant intercourse with the parents.

One of Miss Auld's devices was to place interesting story-books in her bedroom or leave them lying casually in the corners which she frequented. She knew that 'Smoyana cared no longer for light reading. Some time previously when up at Xolobe Mrs. Forsyth had given her a book then popular in Scotland, with the remark, " A friend at home sent this to me, but I am past caring to read anything but the Bible now." Miss Auld was therefore amused to come across her deep in the books she had left, with seeming carelessness, in her way. One evening she found her sitting close up to the window to catch the light of the setting sun in order to finish *The Lady of the Decoration*, which she pronounced " good."

There was a busy fortnight of preparation for the overseas journey; then came a farewell to the people of Mbulu. A meeting was held of the Women's Christian Association, of which she was President. As already stated this society was affiliated to the Upward and Onward organisation, and she had just received from Lady Aberdeen, the President, a friendly personal letter. At the gathering a collection was made as *umpako wendlela*—food for the way—the usual native way of presenting a parting gift. It amounted to £3 : 10s., one old woman, almost eighty, bringing threepence and one elder 2s. She was overcome by their kindness.

When all was over she sighed, and then with the fine spirit of fortitude which had carried her through so many difficult years, she faced, with quiet and steadfast gaze, the dreaded plunge back into civilisation. •

Leaving Paterson at 7 A.M. she and Miss Auld were driven down to the Tsomo River and across the drift in a wagon. On the other side stood a motor-car. She had never seen one before, but without hesitation and without remark she stepped inside. On the way her passport was secured. The filling up of this had caused her considerable amusement. " What is the shape of my forehead ? What kind of nose and mouth have I got ? " she asked helplessly.

## BACK TO CIVILISATION 223

Arriving at Blythswood, that "daughter of Lovedale," a large training and industrial institution, built largely by the gifts of the Fingoes, the motor stopped, and Miss Auld ran in and told the ladies of the mission that Mrs. Forsyth was outside. These went eagerly to greet her and endeavoured to persuade her to stay the night, but she was anxious to finish the first stage of her journey.

At Butterworth the two friends put up at an hotel, and it was remarkable how quickly and without apparent effort the missionary dropped back into the methods of conventional life. Every one was interested in her, and she confided to her companion that she had not found the first step into the world so very dreadful after all.

There was shopping to be done. The boots she wore were still an offence to Miss Auld, and even more so after the remark a lady made when they were put out to be cleaned. "Surely, Miss Auld," she said with a twinkle, "you have a very large husband hidden away somewhere!" A neat comfortable pair was procured, and Miss Auld felt a thrill of triumph when she noticed the flicker of feminine pride which the staid missionary evinced in the improved appearance of her feet.

Next morning a lady walked suddenly in upon them. It was Miss Mann. Aunt and niece met for the first time, and Miss Auld, watching the loving greeting, thanked God that all was well.

" I have motored up from East London," said Miss Mann, " as the train service cannot be depended upon because of troops, so you have only an hour to spare."

But all that the two friends had to say to one another had been said long before.

When the parting came the younger woman stood and watched the brave strong figure pass out of her life, her fluttering bonnet-strings being the last she saw as the car sped swiftly down the street.

And then a picture came into her mind of those thirty lonely years at Xolobe, so quiet and filled with happy and fruitful service; and then another of the future, crowded with new faces and scenes and exciting experiences, and she put up a silent prayer that the aged saint might be dealt with very tenderly and be kept safe and at peace.

# VI

## WAS IT WORTH IT?

As we watch her passing from the scene of her thirty years' toil, one inevitably asks the question, what does such a life and such a service as hers amount to? Were they, as some might think, too restricted in scope? Was it worth spending so long a time wrestling with a few hundreds of heathen? What she accomplished—did it justify the expenditure of so much thought and energy?

So far as visible results are concerned they were neither meagre nor unimportant. Though progress is steady, South Africa is not, perhaps, so fruitful a mission-field as other parts of the continent. A revival is seldom experienced; converts are, as a rule, few; the level of spiritual life is not high. But Mrs. Forsyth had no reason to be dissatisfied with what was achieved in her thirty years' sojourn at Xolobe.

When she arrived the people around her

were pure heathen and as wild and hopeless as any tribe in Africa. Xolobe is now a fully organised mission-station with a fine church building, a day school with four teachers and an attendance of about 140, Sunday services, a Sunday School, a young women's class, and a week-day prayer-meeting, all carried on by the office-bearers she trained. There is also a branch of the Women's Christian Association, the members of which visit the sick and aged from kraal to kraal. Mrs. Forsyth, in short, civilised the district, gave the people a knowledge of God, and brought many scores to the feet of Christ. She had been true to the significance of her Kafir name. " Come . . . O breath," said the prophet, " and breathe upon these . . . that they may live. . . . · And the breath came . . . and they lived."

But neither figures nor organisations present a true estimate of what she performed. Miss Auld sums up the matter rightly when she says : " I think we will never really know the true extent of her work and prayer till that day when all shall be revealed."

For the results attained Mrs. Forsyth herself took not an atom of credit. She held that she was only an instrument; the power and the strength came from above.

## WAS IT WORTH IT? 227

"I desire," she says, "to give all the glory to God for what He has done. Not unto us, Lord, not unto us, but to Thy name be all the glory."

The chief value of her story to those who look on from afar is the example it gives of a life utterly consecrated to the service of Christ. Her abandonment of self, her sacrifice of everything which makes life enjoyable, her humility of spirit, her faith and hope and courage which never failed in the face of the most baffling obstacles and worries, her undimmed freshness of soul amidst the spiritual loneliness and desolation of heathen Africa—all make her stand out as one of the rare and attractive personalities who move and uplift hearts out of the common rut into higher and nobler planes. Her influence cannot die with the cessation of her work; it will live on and spread beyond the confines of Xolobe; it will inspire other wayfaring and struggling souls; it will stimulate and nerve her sister-workers toiling in the mission-fields; and it may bring into a like vocation and sphere some, at least, of those who are, in these new days, dreaming of heroic service.

# VII

## AN ESTIMATE FROM THE FIELD

But a missionary in the field has perhaps the best right to estimate the worth of her character and service, and here is the reasoned opinion of the Rev. Robert Mure of Ross Mission :

" In one sense the contrast between Mrs. Forsyth and other missionaries in the South African field was very great. She had the smallest sphere of any of us—just one station, and even that was under the care of her minister. We missionaries have many stations—fifteen, twenty, even thirty or over. We are superintendents. We ride about like bishops, ordaining, ordering, giving charges, working late and early. No one can call it easy work—and in a sense we are great men in our districts. She was different, a humble figure without charge or function or office in any ecclesiastical sense, ranking as an

## AN ESTIMATE FROM THE FIELD

honorary lay missionary. She had no house to speak of, only a but and a ben, no horse or trap. She simply walked on foot and visited the heathen in their houses close by, and spoke to them of the way of salvation. How different from the missionaries with their large dioceses and much organisation and much travelling and heavy correspondence. Yet, no doubt, she was the most apostolic figure amongst us carrying on a more apostolic work.

" She lived in a remote corner of Fingoland far from the railway and the road and the beaten track. There are tracks to her house, as there are tracks to everywhere in South Africa, made by the feet of savages and by their flocks and herds searching for food, but Xolobe is a dull and lonely spot for a white woman. To live there alone among a few black folk, in a house not much better than theirs, and sharing largely their simple life and simple fare—it was an eccentric thing, perhaps, like that of the new Bush Brotherhood in Australia, but in her case there was no sense of spiritual pride because of ascetic distinction or connection with a great contemplative or historic Order in the Church. She was simply a lone woman, separated by no special function or training or qualification, or churchly ritual, merely a decided and sincere Christian with a great love of souls in her heart, and a deep yearning for the salvation of the heathen. They were in hundreds around her. Heathen men and women and children, likeable, even lovable, in many ways, but grossly ignorant of the best things in life, and without hope for the next life. To her this was a great chance—to be free to live amongst them, and day in, day out, strive to teach them the better way.

" Few can endure such loneliness as hers for very long. Even the most isolated of our unmarried missionaries has a certain and unfailing social solace and variety, his itinerations, his constant dealing with churches and schools and mission agents, and persons in trouble, or needing advice, who visit him daily from one part or another of his district. The missionary's life is really not dull or lacking in intercourse with his fellows by any means.

" But Mrs. Forsyth had none of those social opportunities. She lived at Xolobe for thirty years, month after month and year after year, and daily set her face gladly to the same hard work. She did not throw it up disappointed after five years ; she endured

## AN ESTIMATE FROM THE FIELD 231

it until age and health compelled her to retire. It is unique in our South African mission-field. It is a unique case of the triumph of the soul over a comfortless and heathen environment."

## VIII

## REST TIME

By devious ocean ways and through submarine-infested home waters Mrs. Forsyth came back to her own land and her own city, and looked upon friends and scenes she had not seen for thirty years. From Glasgow she went to Edinburgh to be received by the Foreign Mission Committee of the United Free Church, of which Sir Andrew H. L. Fraser, K.C.S.I., is Convener. That quiet book-lined room has seen many a missionary welcomed home from the ends of the earth, but it is doubtful whether a more interesting figure ever appeared before the Committee than this old lady of Xolobe, with the loneliness of her self-imposed exile clinging to her and giving her a curious air of aloofness.

On a subsequent occasion she was convoyed from Glasgow to Edinburgh by the cousin mentioned in the first chapter, now an active lady of eighty years of age. They

# REST TIME 233

missed one another on returning and Mrs. Forsyth went back alone. In the long dark tunnel she heard a small voice singing softly what seemed at first like some childish rhyme, but by and by she caught the words, " Lord, bless Thy little lamb to-night." It was a little girl who was afraid of the darkness and was singing to comfort herself. Such ingenuous faith touched the heart of the African missionary, and she too comforted herself with the words.

She had much to learn and witness of what had been achieved in the arts of life during her long absence, so that her interest in things was kept fresh and keen. But often the kaleidoscopic scenes about her grew dim, the multitudinous sounds drifted into silence, and she was back in Xolobe with the African sun blazing overhead, the bronze forms of the Fingoes moving about her, and the hum of the children in their wattle-and-daub school murmuring in her ears. . . .

\*    \*    \*    \*    \*

" 'Smoyana," said the writer to her one day in summer when she was sitting looking out upon the beautiful sunlit hills of the homeland, " if you had the chance would you go back and live these thirty years over again at heathen Xolobe?"

"Yes," was the quick but quiet reply, "I should like to do better than I have done."

"But you have done a tremendous lot."

Her eyes filled with tears.

"I have done very little," she said simply. "I should like to do much more before I die."

# INDEX

Africa, South, physical conditions, 20 ; history of, 21
Auld, Rev. Wm., 156, 211, 214, 218, 220
Auld, Miss, 156, 167, 172, 175, 206, 208, 214, 216, 221, 222

Beer-drinking, 75
Bekiwe, 38, 102, 220
"Bella Moir," 106
Bible Class, 85, 161
Buchanan, Rev. J., tribute to Mrs. Forsyth, 109

Cairneyhill, 13, 14, 53, 205

Davidson, Rev. James, 27, 35, 42, 44, 46, 51, 59, 84, 95, 105, 117, 134, 147

Emgwali, 16, 31, 137, 145, 149, 221

Fingo race, origin of, 23 ; character of, 60, 66, 72
Fingoland, 26
Forsyth, Christina, birth, 4 ; conversion, 6; Sunday School teacher, 7 ; love story of, 8, 15, 53; at Cairneyhill, 13 ; voyage to South Africa, 16 ; at Emgwali, 31 ; teacher at Paterson, 35-52 ; marriage, 53 ; return to Paterson, 56 ; arrival at Xolobe, 62 ; adventures, 68 ; opens day school, 81 ;

Forsyth, Christina (contd.)—
siege of the chief, 77 ; starts a Bible Class, 85 ; help from Greenock Ladies' Association, 100 ; the Greenock Schoolhouse, 104 ; Mr. Buchanan's visit, 109 ; arrival of Miss Lamb, 117 ; burning of the church, 121 ; opening of new building, 122 ; school taken over by Government, 132 ; training of boarders, 136 ; doctor's opinion, 138 ; visit of Mr. and Mrs. M'Laren, 140 ; new church, 147 ; opening, 150 ; Mr. Stewart's pen-picture, 151 ; advent of Mr. and Miss Auld, 156 ; personal traits, 169 ; last visit to Paterson, 199 ; her independence, 205 ; the war and her work, 210 ; her nephew killed in action, 212 ; retiral, 216 ; last day at Xolobe, 218 ; arrival at Paterson, 220 ; departure for East London, 224 ; estimate of her work, 225, 228 ; in Scotland, 232

Greenock Ladies' Association, 100, 115 ; winding up of, 144 ; ladies' interest and gifts, 204, 205, 207
Greenock Schoolhouse, 105

Hartley, Dr., tribute, 159

Ida, 108, 136, 145, 165, 217
Initiation ceremonies, 74, 128

Kafirs, origin of, 22; national suicide, 25; characteristics, 28; language, 32
Koti, Candlish, 122, 217

Lamb, Miss, arrival at Xolobe, 117; resignation, 120
Laws, Rev. Dr., 35,

Macfarlane, Miss, 101, 206, 207, 209, 217
M'Laren, Mr. and Mrs., visit to Xolobe, 140; gift of *Mary Slessor*, 213
Mann, Miss, journey to South Africa, 216, 224
Moir, John (father), 4, (son), 13
Mure, Rev. Robert, visit to Xolobe, 201; tribute, 228

Persecution, 83, 87
Polygamy, 73, 161
Prayer, 42, 76

Prayer meetings, 42; for rain, 48, 135

Sclater, Rev. John, 7, 27, 51
Semple, Rev. D. W., 221
'Smoyana, meaning of, 32
Stewart, Rev. George S., arrival 148; pen-picture of Mrs. Forsyth, 151

Taki, troubles with, 88
Thompson, Newton O., opinion of natives, 62; tribute to Mrs. Forsyth, 112

Union of the churches, 139, 143

War, first news of, 210
Witch-doctors, 73, 96, 162

Xolobe, situation, 59, 63; character of people of, 60, 72; Mrs. M'Laren's description, 141; Mr. Stewart's pen-picture, 151; Miss Auld's account, 158; Mr. Mure's description, 202, 229

THE END

*Printed in Great Britain by* R. & R. CLARK, LIMITED, *Edinburgh.*

"Since Blaikie's 'Life of Livingstone' we have had no more inspiring volume about a missionary in the Dark Continent. Mary Slessor was a woman of unique and inspiring personality, and one of the most heroic figures of the age."

# MARY SLESSOR OF CALABAR
Pioneer Missionary
BY W. P. LIVINGSTONE

Price 5s. net.

Dr. Alexander Whyte writes: "The greatest thanks for *Mary Slessor*. We are reading it every evening after dinner with wonder and delight. Mary is worthy to stand beside and before Santa Teresa herself for distinction and originality and devotion and prayer and work. And I can say nothing more than that, for the Spanish Saint is the ablest and the best woman I have met with in all my reading. Your book is an inspiration and a sanctification to read. My daughter, out in the hospital at Alexandria, writes home for good books, and I have sent her the best book I have read for a long time; *one of the best books I ever read.*"

## THE MARY SLESSOR CALENDAR
Compiled by MRS. W. P. LIVINGSTONE

Price 3s. 6d. net.

# THE NEW OUTLOOK
An Ideal of Life of To-Day
BY W. P. LIVINGSTONE

Price 4s. 6d. net.

Men and women are groping after a clearer faith in view of the unsettlement caused by the War. Here, in this book, is the response to the need. The author, standing apart from tradition, presents in simple, non-theological, non-scientific language, a fresh vision of truth, a new and higher ideal of religion. Into what is oldest in the world's thought he weaves, fearlessly, what is newest; examines the principles of life, gives a fresh interpretation of Christ, and applies His teaching, in what is nothing less than a startling way, to the conditions of to-day. It is a book which is sure to have its influence in the time of religious and social reconstruction upon which the world is entering.

HODDER & STOUGHTON, PUBLISHERS, LONDON, E.C. 4.

# SOME NEW BOOKS

## REV. SIR W. ROBERTSON NICOLL

**Reunion in Eternity.** By Sir WILLIAM ROBERTSON NICOLL, Author of "The Church's One Foundation," etc. Price **6s.** net.

This book deals with Reunion. Immortality is assumed as certain. The first part is a series of articles discussing various aspects of Reunion, and analysing the treatment of the subject in Dante, Luther, Melanchthon, Browning, Tennyson, etc. The second part is a series of arranged quotations on the subject chosen from a wide field. The third part contains letters from various authorities. Professor A. S. Peake writes on Reunion as conceived in the Old Testament. Dr. T. E. Page writes on the classical treatment of the subject. The Rev. Canon Barry writes on Reunion as taught by the Church of Rome, and Mr. Arthur Edward Waite writes on Mysticism and Reunion.

## REV. PROFESSOR DAVID S. CAIRNS

**The Reasonableness of the Christian Faith.** By the Rev. Professor DAVID S. CAIRNS, D.D., Author of "Christianity in the Modern World," etc. Price **3s.** net.

## REV. PRINCIPAL A. E. GARVIE

**The Purpose of God in Christ**: And its Fulfilment through the Holy Spirit. By the Rev. Principal A. E. GARVIE, M.A., D.D., Author of "Studies of Paul and his Gospel," etc.
Price **5s.** net.

## DR. JOHN A. HUTTON

**Our only Safeguard.** By the Rev. JOHN A. HUTTON, D.D., Author of "Loyalty the Approach of Faith," etc. Price **6s.** net.

In this volume, directly and indirectly, Dr. Hutton is always moving to the one suggestion that the Christian Faith and a public and private moral obedience in harmony with the Christian Faith are the only safeguards for men's personal progress and refinement, and the only securities for the friendly co-operation of nations and peoples in the collapse of the secular world of the day into general disillusionment and ambiguity. We are directed, too, in many a tone to reconsider the enduring truth and fact of the matter—that "there is no name given under heaven by which men must be saved but the name of Jesus."

## REV. PROFESSOR W. M. CLOW

**Dressed in Beauty not my Own.** By the Rev. Professor W. M. CLOW, D.D., Author of "The Cross in Christian Experience," etc. (Reprinted from "The Evangel of the Strait Gate.")
Price **1s. 3d.** net.

## "BY AN UNKNOWN DISCIPLE"

**By an Unknown Disciple.** Price **6s.** net.

## REV. PROFESSOR A. R. MacEWEN

**The History of the Church in Scotland.** By the Rev. Professor A. R. MacEwen, D.D. The Second Volume. Price **7s. 6d.** net. Professor MacEwen's great work is the "Standard History of the Church in Scotland."

### REVIEWS OF THE FIRST VOLUME.

"Professor MacEwen's eagerly expected work will satisfy the most exacting criticism. A new history of the Church in Scotland has long been urgently wanted, and at length we have it on a scale and in a style worthy of the subject. . . . His narrative is distinguished by a classical clearness and precision, and has all the interest of life." —Professor James Denney in the *British Weekly*. "For a good while past the need for a new history of the Scottish Church has become urgent. . . . Dr. MacEwen has had a great opportunity and has risen to its height. The history of Scottish Christianity has never before been treated with such exactness of knowledge, free from partisanship, and clear discernment of the organic connection of Scottish Church life with the whole political and social development. The style, too, is worthy of the matter."—*Glasgow Herald*. "Professor MacEwen has produced a scholarly volume, which must take its place as the standard work on the subject."—*Scotsman*.

## REV. W. MACKINTOSH MACKAY

**The Disease and Remedy of Sin.** By the Rev. W. MACKINTOSH MACKAY, B.D., Author of "Bible Types of Modern Men," "Bible Types of Modern Women," etc.
Price **7s. 6d.** net.

## REV. JOHN A. IRELAND

**A Legacy from a Scottish Manse.** By the late Rev. JOHN A. IRELAND, Minister of Gartsherrie, Coatbridge. Price **3s. 6d.** net.

The Rev. John A. Ireland fulfilled a ministry of forty-one years in the Church of Scotland. He was ordained at Whitburn in 1876, and fifteen years afterwards was translated to Gartsherrie, Coatbridge, where he ministered until his death in the summer of 1917. When he died, one of our foremost laymen, no mean judge in such a matter, said of him: "He was just about the greatest man of his day in our Church, and scarcely anyone knew him." It is by the kindness of this friend that these papers, which were first addressed to his own people, are now issued in permanent form. Those who did know Mr. Ireland were conscious that he had a gift of original genius, an elemental force of mind and character greater than was manifest in any of his considered acts or utterances ; when he did approximate to perfect self-expression it was most commonly in the heat of extemporaneous discourse. Nevertheless, these papers are highly characteristic of him, and they are now given to a wider public in the hope that those who choose to read them may in some measure be made to share in that mental stimulus and spiritual enrichment which, in his lifetime, he afforded to all who came under his influence.

### REV. PROFESSOR J. H. MOULTON
**The Christian Religion in the Study and the Street.**
By the Rev. Professor JAMES HOPE MOULTON, D.D.
Price **7s. 6d.** net.

All those who knew Dr. J. H. Moulton at all intimately were, sooner or later, struck by the degree to which pure scholarship and evangelistic passion were blended in his nature. Mere painstaking investigation for its own sake had no attraction for him; even grammar was pressed into the service of the Kingdom of God, though he would have deprecated the imputation of incongruity implied in the statement. Side by side with his Greek Testament studies he pursued eager enquiries in the field of comparative religion—the result of philological studies during his college days under the inspiring leadership of Professor E. B. Cowell. The choice of material for this volume has been influenced by the desire to represent his twofold interest in the more or less academic study of the records of Christianity, and the practical work of Christianity on the field which is the world.

### DR. WILLIAM M. MacGREGOR
**Repentance Unto Life:** And the Life it leads to. By WILLIAM MALCOLM MACGREGOR, D.D., St. Andrew's United Free Church, Edinburgh. Price **6s.** net.

The complaint has often been made against evangelical preaching that it is so occupied with the question of a right beginning as to have little to say about the good life. Perpetually and suitably it keeps saying, "Come," but it does not enlarge upon what men find who come. In Rabbi Duncan's image it is an open door without a palace behind to which it gives admission. In the twenty-eight discourses which compose this volume an attempt is made to supply both. Much is said of the call and of the forces which keep men, from answering it, and of the joy of those who have heard; but illustration is also given, step by step, of the way in which the new life grows, in integrity and regard for others, in prayer and rest of heart, until it is completed in the Life Everlasting.

### REV. PROFESSOR J. H. MOULTON and
### REV. PROFESSOR GEORGE MILLIGAN
**The Vocabulary of the Greek Testament.** By the Rev. Professor J. H. MOULTON, D.D., D.C.L., and the Rev. Professor G. MILLIGAN, D.D. Complete in six parts. Parts I. and II., already published. Part III., to be published this Autumn.
Price **7s. 6d.** net.

### REV. A. B. MACAULAY, M.A., and
### REV. F. J. PAUL, M.A., B.D.
**Up against It: Questions the Boys are asking.** By the Rev. A. B. MACAULAY, M.A., and the Rev. F. J. PAUL, M.A., B.D.
Price **5s.** net.

HODDER & STOUGHTON, PUBLISHERS, LONDON, E.C. 4.

PLEASE DO NOT REMOVE
CARDS OR SLIPS FROM THIS POCKET

UNIVERSITY OF TORONTO LIBRARY

H&SS
A
5821

CPSIA information can be obtained
at www.ICGtesting.com
Printed in the USA
LVOW10s0235140917
548700LV00020B/762/P